The PsychoKitty Speaks Out

Diary Of A Mad Housecat

The PsychoKitty Speaks Out
Diary Of A Mad Housecat

Published by Inkblot Books

Vacaville California

www.inkblotbooks.com

ISBN 1-932461-07-8

Published in the Untied States Of America

The PsychoKitty Speaks Out

Diary Of A Mad Housecat

Max Thompson

Giving a voice to kitties everywhere

I'm Max.
I'm 14 pounds of sleek black and white glory.
With an attitude.
And opinions.
On everything.

OCTOBER 25, 2003

Something interesting: my entire nose fits into just one of the Woman's nostrils. She gets all pissy on me when I do this, but what does she realistically expect? I mean, come on! Something up there smells like it buried itself in deep and died. It's putrid, foul, and disgusting smelling.

I.
Love.
It.

It's not like I bother her every ten minutes for catch a whiff. Out of common courtesy I wait until she's asleep. I creep very carefully onto her sleeping body, sit gently, and jam my nose up the closest nostril as far—and as delicately—as I can. It's not as if I'm *trying* to wake her up. It's not my fault if she a) sleeps too lightly, and b) has this thing about me standing on her boobs.

I don't know about these People. I've already made it clear that cats don't love people, but the Woman keeps picking me up and cooing "I knoooowwwww you lovvvve me."

Look, lady, you *paid* someone to cut my nads off. No, I don't love you. Besides, if you really loved *me*, you wouldn't get so bent out of shape when I stand outside the bedroom door at 3 a.m. to sing. I have a good voice—you should sit up, listen, and appreciate the gift of my musical talent.

Oh, and tell the Man that if he ever locks me in the bathroom again, I'm going to poop on his pillow.

October 26, 2003

Ok, let's start with today's "time change." I don't care what the people say, it was a BAD IDEA. Sure, their fancy little timepieces might have said 7 a.m., but my *stomach* said it was 8 a.m. and *that's the latest I should be forced to wait for food.* I'm not a bad cat. Most mornings I wait patiently for the Woman to drag herself out of bed before I begin my daily reminders that I haven't been fed since the night before and I am Starving To Death.

This time change is an egregious error. I was not about to wait until one of the People decided they'd had enough rest. I was hungry, dammit, so of *course* I started calling out to them. Gently at first. Naturally. But when they were still wrapped up in those blankets and my stomach was growling so hard it hurt, I let them have it. Yes, I howled my freaking head off, until the Man finally got up.

But would he lower himself to opening up a can of Stinky Goodness for me? No. He read his stupid newspaper first.

Look, people, get a clue. We don't love you. We love your opposable thumbs. Accept that and we'll get along much better.

October 27, 2003

A common misconception among those chosen to care for our species: when we wind our way through your legs while you are trying to walk down stairs, we are not trying to kill you. That would be counterproductive; if you die, who will open the cans of food?

Really, we're only trying to piss you off. And it seems like we're doing a very good job.

October 28, 2003

In what world is it acceptable to come home an hour and fifteen minutes late when you have a hungry feline waiting for you? Okay, so it was really only fifteen minutes late, but I'm still extremely annoyed about this time change. Yeah, sure, the People always leave dry food out, but they *know* that's not what I want.

I'm not obsessed with food. It just seems that way.

And what's with this "No, you can't sit on my lap right now?" bull? I don't care if you have to pee. Hold it and let me have my throne.

Oh yeah, and if you don't change my litter box tonight, I'm going to poop on your pillow.

OCTOBER 29, 2004

Peoples, thou must remembereth: if you pisseth off the cat, something you own may meet a toothy death.

Just a thought…

OCTOBER 30, 2004

Here's a DUH moment for you.
I barf, and the Woman comes up and asks, "Aw, do you have a tummy ache?"

Hello?
Do you not see the contents of my tummy all over the kitchen floor?

Clean it up—without yakking your own dinner up—and feed me again.
My tummy *did* hurt…now it's just empty.

OCTOBER 31, 2003

All right, I was just lying there on the chair, licking myself, when the Woman comes up, picks me up *without asking*, and hugs me while cooing "Ooooh, you are so cute."

Well, yeah, lady I *know* that, but come on.
Just, geez.
Gag me.

~~~

People traditions are just odd. And annoying. You'd never find a bunch of cats throwing costumes on and going door to door, begging for treats they're normally not allowed to have. It was sad, really, to see all these small humans posturing their imagined cuteness for candy that neither smells bad enough to be good nor reeks enough to get them high.

Amateurs.

Cats never beg. We demand. And we usually get what we want.

Take tonight, for instance. My people were sitting outside with the neighbors and their small, sticky male offspring. I was hungry—it was only half an hour until dinner time, and my stomach was rumbling loudly—so every time one of them came into the house for one thing or another, I hollered at them.

And what do you know, after my incessant demands (and some forced cuteness; I don't mind the small sticky person so much, and I'll humor him by letting him wave at me through the screen, which seems to make them all happy) the Woman ran inside—yes, she *ran*—to fill my plate with some nice Trout Stinky Goodness.

Begging doesn't work.

But demanding, in a tone that says, "This is my right, and you are my servant," invariably does.

People are so gullible.

November 1, 2003

Attention, fellow felines ... if you live in a house with stairs (the more the better) this is a must-do:

Take a golf ball, or some other hard rolling object, and carry it to the top-most stair. Set it down, and push it over the edge. Listen as it loudly bounces down the stairs *thunk-thunk-thunk-thunk* and then a nice *whirrrrr* as it rolls across the floor at the bottom.

Run down stairs, as heavy footed as you can, get the ball, and run back up.

Repeat the process.

Trust me, your People will love this.

~ ~ ~

The Woman was sitting here at the desk, typing away, when I jumped up into her lap to see what she was working on. She looked down and asked, "Do you mind?"

I was thinking, "No, not really, just keep on doing it," but she sighed and lifted me up, then plopped me down onto the seat, muttering something about having to answer Mother Nature.

I didn't even hear the phone ring.

NOVEMBER 2, 2003

Felines have very sensitive hearing; this isn't just a personal affliction, it's a scientific fact. We hear better than humans do, and certain noises are not only unpleasant, they're downright painful.

Bearing this in mind, people, please *stop singing*.
You don't sound half as good as you think.
In fact, you don't sound good at all.

So, stop. Just stop.

NOVEMBER 3, 2003

Holy crap, how much can one person pee?
Really, if she were using my litter box, it would have exploded by now.
At this rate, she might as well just sleep in the bathroom.
Just…wow.

NOVEMBER 4, 2003

We used to have a dog. He was there when the Younger Human (where the hell did he go, anyway?) brought me home; I admit, at first I was terrified of him, but he made it clear right from the bat that he didn't intend to turn me into kitty cacciatore, so we kept our separate peace. He fulfilled his position of being the family gas bag, and since The People were so absorbed in the vast quantities of fur he shed all over the place, they rarely noticed how much I was leaving on their clothes and furniture. He left me alone, so all in all he was all right for a dog.

No, cats and dogs don't always hate each other. We can co-exist, and I under-stand that my feline predecessor treated the dog as if he was her own child. A little weird, but, whatever.

He's gone, too, now, though I'm pretty sure he's not off with the Younger Human; my People can talk about the Younger Human in the present tense, but they talk about the dog with sadness tinged voices. As if Something Happened. Something not very good.

This afternoon the Woman was looking at a picture of herself and the dog while I bathed on the window perch in her office. She glanced over at me and said, "I still miss my Booger Bear, Max."

I could point out that she has her species a little mixed up, but I won't; she did seem genuinely sad and in need of something. I can never be sure what 'some-thing' it is that people need, but they seem to enjoy it if I spend a few minutes on their laps, so I abandoned the bath and jumped up in her lap and did the cute thing—you know, standing up on my back legs and rubbing my face against hers. It's demeaning, but what the hell, it does seem to make her happy.

I gave a little purr and let her pet me a little, and didn't bite when she rubbed my tummy (people, get a clue, we usually bite because we hate that...)

She seemed happier after that.
I even got fed my dinner 45 minutes early.

It's something to remember; tolerate a little of their fawning in exchange for food.
Works for me.
But I don't love them.
Nope.

~~~

You know, in spite of what the People say, I'm not really a wuss. Yes, I enjoy lying on my special window seats and staring at everything going on outside, but that doesn't mean I want to *go* outside. Why would I? There are Sticky Little People outside, little creatures who would pull my tail and grab at my fur, while shrieking and screaming, and I have no desire to be that close to them.
There are also DOGS out there. I see them—the dog across the street, that white furry thing everyone calls "Lucky." You might think he's trained and

well behaved, but if I put a shock collar on you, you'd do whatever I wanted, too. And face it, shock collar or not, if he wanted to take a bite out of me, he would.

And I've seen those birds. Those suckers are *huge*. We're not talking dainty little sparrows here, we're talking football sized crows. You have to respect a bird that could lift up one of those small Sticky People and carry it off. They outweigh me. I see the odds.

But that doesn't mean I'm a wuss, or chicken, or a 'fraidy cat. It means I have brain, for Pete's sake. Inside I have food almost on demand, several warm beds, several window seats, two laps to choose from, and a litter box that's cleaned on an almost regular basis. Why would I want to go out there when I have all this in here?

November 5, 2003

He took me outside! The Man picked me up and took me out the front door, where he (with the help of the Woman…I'll remember that) allowed one of those Sticky Little People to come up to me. While he held me tight he told the kid that he could touch me! Holy freaking overflowing litter box!

When he's not looking, I am going to poop on his pillow.

November 6, 2003

Well, I tried. I had my chance this morning to get even with the Man for taking me outside, but it didn't quite work. I had him on the stairs at 4:30 in the morning, and wound between his legs, even stood on my back legs and pawed at him, but he kept his balance.

I was nicer to the Woman; she was still sleeping when my stomach started growling, so I just jumped up on the bed and waited, patiently, curled up on her back. It didn't take long, and she was duly grateful for the extra few minutes of snoozing. She didn't take too long getting down the stairs and fed me right off the bat.

She did scowl at me later—the Man phoned home and tattled on me, told her I'd tried to kill him on the stairs. Phfft. If I'd really wanted him dead… She reminded me that he's the one who pays for my food, especially the most awesome cans of Stinky Goodness.

Well, fine. I won't try to kill him, but I'm not going to curl up and kiss his ass, either. At some point he'll figure out that feeding me is his *honor*.

One can hope.

November 7, 2003

She's baking something she calls "brownies" and holy crud, they smell awesome. But I guarantee, when they're done, she'll declare "these aren't good for kitties."

Yeah, well, lady, judging from the size of your ass, they're not good for you, either.

November 8, 2003

Ok. You come home, I jump in your lap, you pet me, and then remark, "Damn, your fur is cold."

Doesn't that inspire a light bulb moment for you?

Turn up the freaking heat! Just because I have a fur coat, that doesn't mean I want icicles hanging off my already-useless nipples!

November 9, 2003

Cripes.
Lady, that's not music.
Music is me singing to you at three in the morning.
That stuff…whatever "Ozzie" is, "Ozzie" is not music.
"Ozzie" is one step down from a dog whistle.
"Ozzie" hurts my ears.
Stop.
Now.

November 10, 2003

You know, I try to be helpful. As annoying as humans are, they feed me (and yeah, as hard as it is to admit, they feed me well), and change the litter box with acceptable frequency. So I try to do my bit, but do they appreciate it in return?

Hell no.

Take this morning. The Man gets up early most mornings and wanders off for the better part of the day. I know he hates it when the alarm clock goes off, so I try to get up the stairs a little before that happens, and I sing for my People. It's better to wake to music, isn't it?

Do they like it?

Hell no.

I stood out there in the hall, singing at the top of my lungs, and what did I get?

"Stop it, Max."
"Be quiet Max."
"Dammit, Max, *shut up.*"

He did get up, and he did make it out the door at his usual time, but do I get any thanks?

Hell no.

Ingrates.

NOVEMBER 11, 2003

I wonder if the Woman realizes that when she's sitting at the computer, between bouts of typing, that she picks really gross things out of her ears? And that she flicks them to the floor?

Whatever it is, it does *not* taste good.

NOVEMBER 12, 2003

The Woman was taking a break from typing today (well, I think she was surfing online, but she tries to make everyone think she's working) and I jumped on her lap; she was staring at the wall near the ceiling and said, "Someday when we have our own place, we're going to put walkways up really high for you to wander around the house on."

Well, first, why wait for "someday?" That sounds freaking cool.

And second…this isn't our own place?

Who's is it? And what if they want us to leave?

NOVEMBER 13, 2003

My People were up very, very early today; it wasn't terribly early for the Man, but it was Way Too Early for the Woman. And no matter what they tell you, it wasn't my fault. I kept my mouth shut this morning, I didn't sing for them, and I didn't stand in the middle of her chest trying to smell the inside of her nose (though I really would like to, as it smells especially obnoxious today.)

No, they were up, I think, because there was no electricity. The Woman can't sleep without a fan going, and this *thing* in the hallway kept chirping. It was loud, annoying, and hurt my ears.

He walked out the front door, yelling back something about wind and freaking cold, and she provided a warm lap for me, which truth be told I appreciated because it really was getting cold. I let her read the comics by flashlight, and when it was light outside, she fed me early, very early, and went back to bed.

Of course, the phone rang just a little while later and woke her up, but by then I was full and sleepy, all curled up in the blankets on her bed, so what do I care?

She even gave me my dinner early.

That means I can start bugging her for breakfast at 6 a.m. tomorrow.

NOVEMBER 14, 2003

Vacuums should be illegal.

NOVEMBER 15, 2003

Want to know why I crawled up on your chest and blocked your view of the TV? Because I was watching it, and you came in and changed the freaking channel. Yes, once in a while I like to watch Animal Planet. And when this once in a blue moon event comes along, you do not have the right to plop

down on the bed and put it on the news! There is nothing happening anywhere in the world more important than watching stupid dogs do stupid things
to their stupid owners. Seriously. What could be better than seeing some ankle
biter yowling while his owner insists he's saying, "I love you?"

Note to people: those dogs aren't saying they love you. They're saying, "I want
steak."

November 16, 2003

Um, yeah, I do have a potty mouth.
Is that a problem?

November 17, 2003

I do not "beg."
I request.
Loudly
Frequently.
But I do not "beg."

November 18, 2003

She thinks she's spoiling me. She insinuated it in a sarcastic sort of way, in any
case. I was sitting on the ottoman, waiting (patiently, I might add, no matter
what she thinks about the 15 times I tried to crawl into her lap, stick my head
up her pants legs, and head butt her thigh) for her to get up and go into the
other room—it was time, after all; I *always* get to sleep in the comfy chair after
the news is over—and when she did actually stand up, she then lifted me from
where I was at to the seat she had so considerately warmed for me.

Her comment? "I don't spoil you, do I?"

Hey, I'm not stupid. I know a snotty rhetorical question when I hear one. It's
right up there with, "Are you hungry?" first thing in the morning.

Hey, lady, how about a nice, *"Well, **duh!**"*

People...

November 19, 2003

It is seriously, seriously unfair to pick the exact moment that I really need to use the litter box to clean it. Even more unfair to take over a minute to do it. The Woman is lucky I didn't poop on the nice white rug in the bathroom instead.

I still might, just to show how irritated I am.

November 20, 2003

Getting out the vacuum when I'm trying to inform the world that it's dinner time isn't just mean, it's vicious. The People evidently thought that would shut me up for a while, but as soon as they put the sucky monster away, I crept out from under the table and started reminding them again. Loudly. Repetitively.

They got just as repetitious.
"Not now, Max."
"It's not time, Max."
"You have over an hour, Max."

It's time for the People to expand their vocabularies.
Or to just shut up and feed me when I ~~ask~~ demand.

People talk too much, really.

November 21, 2003

I found something today that's great fun.

If your human has just had something bubbly to drink, and they're lying on the floor, you can jump on their tummy and make them belch.

After they belch, run up to their head and smell their breath. You can tell what they've had to eat for the last three or four days. Plus they're too busy moaning and holding their tummy to stop you from getting a really good sniff.

November 22, 2003

Just because I don't want to eat what you might have, that doesn't mean I don't want to sniff it.

Take cottage cheese, for instance. I don't want to eat that crap, but if you have some, I'd like to take a sniff. You know, just in case. It might have turned into something palatable.

NOVEMBER 23, 2003

Oh, man, the Woman was cooking something that smelled *really* good this afternoon... it was like meat, but it was round and flat. And it smelled different as she was frying it up—like bacon, only not.

I worked it hard, trying to get her to give me some, but—big surprise—she wouldn't. She just muttered something about "fried bologna would hurt your tummy," but I don't buy it, not one bit.

She just didn't want to share.
Sometimes I think they do these things just to be mean.
That would be a People kind of thing to do.

NOVEMBER 24, 2003

Don't ask me how much I think I can eat in a day. I've never been given the opportunity to figure that one out, so asking me is like being a giant walking tease. Yeah, you. You're a food tease. And a mean one at that.

NOVEMBER 25, 2003

The Woman is a Cat Slut. She cheated on me, I know she did! She came home today and smelled like some other kitty. I'm not kidding! This is worse than coming home smelling like a dog. I mean...another cat? Why? Oh, *she* says she just picked up a kitty and petted it and then put it right back down, but you don't get that kitty smell by just stroking one for a second or two. You have to really get into it. I may never get over this.

NOVEMBER 26, 2003

How's this for unfair? The People cooked this dinner last night that smelled like it should be mine. Very meaty, the aroma was all over the house. But did I get any?

Hell no.

The woman looks down at me and apologizes, saying that if I ate any, in ten minutes I'd have flames shooting out my ass.

So what?

I don't know what onions are and I don't care, but dammit if you're going to cook something that smells like that, you better give me some. I mean it. Next time, you better give me some, or I really am going to poop on your pillow.

NOVEMBER 27, 2003

Think it's funny that sometimes when I sleep my tongue hangs out and you can see part of my inner eyelids? Well, do you want the world to know what *you* look like when you're asleep? Trust me, it ain't pretty.

NOVEMBER 28, 2003

Yesterday was a very good day. It was like *the People finally **get** it!* The Woman spent hours preparing a perfectly wonderful meal, just for me. It damn near drove me nuts, having to be patient and wait through all the smells drifting through the air, and then while the People taste tested everything to make sure it was perfect. Once they were satisfied that the meal was up to par, they both cut up the meat into bite size pieces for me, and even added these slimy (but very tasty) noodles to my plate.

And today! There was more! Again they tasted it first to make sure it was good enough (though I don't know why—it's not as if it changed from yesterday); while they ate I stood on my perch and stared at the Man, aiming my thoughts at his head (and worried that his skull might be a tad too dense), mentally chanting, "mine, mine, mine."

Again, it was very tasty. They also ate this orangey-looking thing that smelled like it was something I would want, but neither offered any to me. That was okay—this time. I was quite stuffed from the turkey and noodles.

Now I wonder what's on the menu for tomorrow. It's about time that they finally started giving me the sustenance I deserve.

NOVEMBER 29, 2003

Why do I go right back to bed after breakfast? Well, getting someone with those nifty opposable thumbs out of bed to open a can is hard work. Seriously.

It takes an hour or more to get one of them up sometimes. After work that hard, a cat needs a nap. If a person wants a cat to stay awake, then a person should get up at the first, "Please, I'm hungry." I'm just sayin'…

November 30, 2003

I don't care if your ass hurts and your legs are going numb.
If I'm napping on your lap, stay there until I'm done.
It's not like you have anything better to do.

December 1, 2003

Is it too much to ask, that when I'm napping, the People be quiet? None of this laughing or talking loudly or playing the TV too loud. Just. Be. Quiet.

I only nap for about 18 hours a day, so I don't think that's being overly demanding.

December 2, 2003

Jingle balls?
For me?
Come on, what am I—two?

Now turn around and go away, and if you hear tinkling, it's only because I'm moving them to a different part of the house. Somewhere I don't have to see them and be reminded of how juvenile you think I am.

Really now.
JINGLE balls…

December 3, 2003

Cream of wheat, I've discovered, is a pretty tasty dish. Even tastier when the Woman has set it down and walks away from it long enough for me to get a quick sample.

It was a little too warm for my liking, but overall, not too bad. The texture is a little strange though. Almost sand papery.

Kind of like my tongue.
Yum.

DECEMBER 4, 2003

Tonight I was nearly killed by Human Female Butt. A vast amount of human female butt, I might add. The Woman has developed the annoying habit of sitting on the sofa at the precise moment I am jumping from the high kitchen counter onto it, and she even picks the same cushion I'm aiming for.

One of these days I'm not going to be able to scramble out from under that looming mass and wind up nothing but a black and white smear on the pleather of life.

DECEMBER 5, 2003

They locked me in the bathroom! Not once, not twice, but just about every freaking day this week. I didn't do anything wrong; I was just minding my own business, curled up on the chair, when the Woman grabbed me and shoved me into the little downstairs bathroom.

And she obviously had been planning on this, as there was food and water and a bed already waiting for me in there. But *why?* I didn't poop on her pillow. I didn't bring some dead thing into her bed. I bit her, sure, but only on the top of her head, and only by accident (I was licking her hair, it smelled really good, and I just wanted to see if it also tasted good.) I didn't mean for it to hurt.

She muttered things about Strange People in the house and Ceiling Fans and Loud Noises, but what does that have to do with punishing *me?*

The food and the bed are still in the bathroom. Not a good sign. I need to hide for the rest of the day, just in case…

DECEMBER 6, 2003

You are never going to believe it. I mean, I still don't. After all the crap this week, all the noise and strange people and getting locked in the bathroom for hours on end, what happens?

She locked me in the freaking closet!

Not just for a minute or two, but for over *two hours.* In the fricking *dark.*

Really, what did I do that was so awful? Why am I being punished every single day? I'm sweet, I'm personable, and I'm pretty. Why am I being treated so horribly???

DECEMBER 7, 2003

I can get the poop out of my own ass, thank you very much. You don't need to chase me around the house with a wad of toilet paper in hand, squealing, "Hold still and let me get it! Hold still and let me get it!"

Leave me alone, and eventually it will fall out on its own, or I'll scoot across the carpet and nudge it out, and then you can play with it all you want.

Sheesh, people...get a little dignity.

DECEMBER 8, 2003

Um, yes, if it hits the floor I *do* think it's mine. It's not like you'll eat it now, so I might as well. And no, I don't care about flames shooting out my ass or noxious eruptions emanating from my various bodily orifices. If you drop food on the floor, even hot peppers, it's mine. Taking it away before I can get to it just is not fair.

DECEMBER 9, 2003

Here's one of the cardinal rules: rub my tummy, especially if I don't expect it, and expect to have my teeth sink deeply into your hand.

If you want to rub a tummy, get a dog.

Well, no, don't. Just don't ever touch my tummy again unless I specifically invite you to.
That will happen approximately 5.7 seconds after Hell freezes over.

DECEMBER 10, 2003

In today's email:

An offer for a mortgage at 3 percent. If I ever find out what that is, I just might accept.

Someone wants my bank account number so they can give me millions and millions of dollars. This wasn't Nigerian President Mumbo Jumbo, but the wife of some dead guy. I'm sorry her husband is dead, but she shouldn't go around offering to give strange kitties all his money. I'm sure he had other plans for it.

A genuine Ro.Lex watch. Sure. Like I care what time it is, unless my tummy is growling.

I'm waiting for a credit card offer. I found a place online that sells stuff *just* for kitties. I bet I could buy lots of fresh kitty crack there.

DECEMBER 11, 2003

Can you believe it! They brought a *tree* into the house! It's fricking huge, too, going all the way up to the ceiling. It's like my own personal wet dream. A tree of my own!

I've spent my whole life looking out the window at trees, and they've always appealed to me. I know birds spend quite a bit of time sitting in trees, so my hopes are pretty high that sooner or later one will pop out—snack time!

What I don't get is why they put all these shiny things on it. They're fun to play with (even though I get yelled at) but the tree would have been awesome without them. The Man put lots of bright lights on it, and the Woman put on the shiny dangling things. I had loads of fun playing last night while they were asleep (a good time to play, because they can't yell at you then.)

And I haven't tried it yet, but they put the little sofa close to the tree, so I can make a leap from it to the top of the tree—just in case that bird shows up.

The only problem, as I see it…that tree tastes *nothing* like I expected it to.

DECEMBER 12, 2003

Dear Baby Jesus,

My taste buds are still all a-twitter from that really good meal the Woman made for me a couple of weeks ago. I've been asking nicely to have that meal repeated, but she just doesn't get it. It's like we're speaking two different languages. So, could you put the thought into her head that cooking it again would be a Very Good Thing?

Thank You,
Max, age 2

DECEMBER *13, 2003*

Rose are red
Violets are blue
Feed me right now
Or I'll poop on you.

DECEMBER *14, 2003*

What's the point of having a tree in the house if you're not allowed to climb it? I mean, come on.

And what's with the white stuff falling out of the sky and covering the ground? It's kind of pretty, but it sure didn't make the Woman very happy. In fact, she even said a few choice words about it, grumbling a whole heck of a lot until she peeked out the window. Someone, she says, shoveled the driveway for her. Whatever the hell that means. But it made her happy, happy enough that she sat down to watch TV and let me stretch out across her lap for a long nap.

She's warm when I need her to be. It would be nice if she'd get up in the morning when I want her to.

DECEMBER *15, 2003*

I was lounging in the living room and the Woman had the TV on, and I noticed a kitty on the TV. She was being given some Stinky Goodness in a beautiful crystal dish. It was beautiful—all bright and shiny, and it made the Stinky Goodness look that much better.

So why do I get mine on an icky old white and black plate? I'm a good kitty. Where's my freaking crystal?

DECEMBER *16, 2003*

Just because I occasionally get into the bathtub, that doesn't mean I want you to turn the water on. It's just a place to sit, and when it's hot in the house, the bottom of the tub feels nice and cool. I do not need you to give me a bath; I'm perfectly capable of managing that on my own.

And really, *why* do you get in and turn water on? I promise you, you'd get just as clean by licking yourself off, and then you wouldn't have to turn around and clean your own bodily scum out of the tub.

Cat baths are just more efficient. You should try it.

DECEMBER 17, 2003

It occurs to me, that if you should fail to clean my litter box in a timely manner, that I don't *have* to poop on your pillow.

You have LOTS of things I can poop on.
And hidden places I can poop in.
Places you won't even think about, at least not until the smell settles in.

DECEMBER 18, 2003

Is it necessary to comment on the speed with which I consume my meals? Really. Okay, sure, the chicken you had for dinner and shared (after much pleading on my part) was very good, but you didn't give me a whole lot, so of course it was gone fairly quickly. You don't have to make an issue of it, nor do you need to declare me a fur-covered food vacuum.

Face it, when your portions are generally less than 2 ounces, the food is going to be gone in short order. You try it. See how you like it.

DECEMBER 19, 2003

Hey, those white hairs on the computer keyboard aren't necessarily mine. Lady, have you looked in the mirror lately? I'm seeing quite a bit of hair on you that isn't dark colored…

DECEMBER 20, 2003

Oooh. Shrimpy Goodness.
Mmmm.
The Man shared, and nicely, so it's now naptime…

December 21, 2003

Rolling a bottle cap on the floor is not going to distract me from trying to remind you that my tummy is growling and you need to get up and feed me.

It will, however, give me the idea that I should place it somewhere you're sure to step on in the middle of the night when you're not wearing shoes.

December 22, 2003

They're screwing with my mind.

A few days ago they left—at night—and came back hours later with two people. I wasn't too sure about them at first, but then I realized underneath all that hair that one of them was the Younger Human. The one who first brought me home. I recognized his smell, but I didn't recognize the other person. I'll tell you what, she smells better than he does, that's for sure.

These younger people, they know how to treat me. He plays with me the right way—he knows how to swing my toy through the air so I can jump up to attack it (nothing personal to my Other People, but chasing things along the floor is, well, *boring*.) And she doesn't grab me and hold me in her lap when I don't want to be held. She lets me sniff her hand and decide if I'm in the mood to be petted.

It occurs to me…maybe my People are just too old for me.

In any case, I like the young people. They can stay.

December 23, 2003

I'm still young. I still have energy. I still need to expend that energy before I implode.

So why do the People get bent when I run up and down the hall and stairs, over and over and over? If they're so worried about being bowled over then they need to just stay out of the hall and off the stairs.

Simple.

DECEMBER *24, 2003*

Every cat needs a high perch like this to oversee all his People.

Supreme Commander Kitty Tower
Make sure your People get you one.

DECEMBER *25, 2003*

This time I didn't really mean to bite the Woman. It's just that she'd obviously been handling some sort of food, and I could smell it, and it smelled like it was tasty…so I tried to take a bite.

As soon as I tasted gross human grime I took my mouth off her, but she acts like I tried to rip her spleen out or something.

Really, she would know if I'd been trying to take an actual bite.

There would be blood.
And screaming.
And…blood.

Something unusual. The People stayed home all day yesterday. That never happens; someone always disappears for a little while, but they were here all day yesterday, and spent a decent amount of time entertaining me. And food! The Woman cooked for me again, just like she did about a month ago.

They started early in the morning (well, early for them, it was kind of late for me.) The Woman got up and fed me (perfectly stinky stuff, very gratifying) and read the paper for a little while, and then the Man came home from where ever it is he goes most days and some nights. Once he was there the Younger Humans came downstairs and they started digging around in these freakishly huge socks that have been hanging on the wall—the dang things were stuffed with goodies, even new toys for me. While they did that the Woman had stuff in the oven for their breakfast—of which I got *nothing*, and it smelled pretty good, too.

Then the fun started. They've had all these shiny boxes under the tree (I am still not allowed to climb) for a couple of weeks now. It was pretty and all, but they were getting in my way...well, yesterday morning they started handing the shiny boxes to each other and ripped the coverings off. That was wicked awesome—they balled up the coverings and threw them across the room for me, so I could chase them and leap over the chairs and stuff.

And then there were boxes! Most of them were too small for me to climb in, but I at least gave it a shot. At one point I think they had six boxes on the floor for me. The last box was really big; the Younger Human, the one with all the hair all over his head and face, opened it up and took its innards out for me, and that was a blast to climb in. It still had some balled up newspaper in it, all the better to dig around in.

It was quiet for a while after that, but then the aroma started settling in the air. Baby Jesus came through—she was doing it, she was making me another turkey! And those slimy noodles! Really, the only thing missing was something fishy, but I've heard her say she doesn't "do" fish. Phfft. I like her, but she does have a serious personality defect. Who *doesn't* want fish???

Anyway.

It was a busy day all around, what with all the paper and boxes I had to play with, and later on the hairy Younger One and his Much Better Smelling Friend helped me play with my new toys. I was so tired I forgot to get up at 3:30 this morning to sing to them. I think I slept in until almost 8 o'clock, and the Woman was very happy to see me jump up on the bed to remind her I needed breakfast. I mean, she actually got out of bed and went downstairs to get me food before she made her bed or changed her clothes. That, like, *never* happens.

I think it was my birthday or something. It should happen more often.

DECEMBER *27, 2003*

Woman, I am not trying to kiss you. I am trying to smell your breath. You obviously ate something tasty, and I want to know what it is so I can go into the kitchen and see if there's any of it left. Just let me sniff, and stop trying to kiss me back. 'Cause it's not a kiss! It's not!

DECEMBER *28, 2003*

If today is the first day of the rest of your life, I think I'd like to start the rest of my life with a big bowlful of real live dead cooked meat...

MONDAY, DECEMBER *29, 2003*

Shrimp!
Shrimp!
Shrimp!

They're fricking huge, in the refrigerator, and I want them!

I mean, these things are beautiful. They must have 20 of them, all bigger than one of my forepaws. All pink and pretty, and surely very juicy. They *have* to be for me. Right? *Right???*

I've been asking for at least one since 7:30 this morning, but will anyone bother?

Phfffft.

DECEMBER 30, 2003

I don't mind, usually, if the People wander off for a good part of the day, especially if it's a gloomy day. All I really want to do on gloomy days is sleep, anyway.

But, People, if you *do* leave and you're not coming back until late, leave me at least one light on. Just one. That's all I ask. Something I can use to get my bearings with.

If you don't, next time you come home, instead of sitting just far enough away from the front door that your foot misses me, I'll make sure I'm positioned right where you'll trip over me. And then you'll think, "Dammit, if only I had left a light on, I would have *seen* him...!"

DECEMBER 31, 2003

Yeah, so what if I was in the same spot when you left the house 12 hours ago? Is there a law that says I have to move? Why would I? That was a comfy spot, and if you hadn't disturbed the peaceful aura around it, I would still be there, still comfy and warm and sleepy.

JANUARY 1, 2004

Sometimes the Woman tells me about the dreams she has, and lemme tell ya, they're never any good. It seems like something horrible always happens: she's naked in school or she's running through the house with a sword and trips, spearing my beautiful little body, or aliens attack and she has to save the world but can't. Or she's running through the house carrying me and runs smack into a wall, splattering my little brains all over the white paint. *Or*, she dreams that she can't find me, and she's terrified that someone has let me out and I'm now just road kill (there's a pattern to her dreams, I'm thinking...)

Know what I dream about? I dream about bowls filled with shrimp, real live dead fish, steak and hamburger and other dead cow things. Once in a while I dream about being a giant kitty, with sharp claws and human verbal skills, and overtaking the world, but that's still a good dream. In the end I always get the good food, and more than I can eat.

I think the Woman needs to have a better bedtime snack. If she'd eat more stinky stuff, she wouldn't have any bad dreams. And she'd smell so much better.

Lady, *you* bought the extra big container of kitty litter. *You* thought you'd save money by buying a 37 pound container instead of the usual 14 pound container. So don't bitch at *me* because cleaning my box is a pain in the butt now. Just clean it, and get out of my way.

And yes, I *do* need to do that just as soon as you finish cleaning it.
Every time.

JANUARY 3, 2004

I like to get up on the table sometimes, mostly because I know the Man doesn't like it. So when he's not here, I jump up and wiggle my butt all over it, especially near the place he sits. Then, when he's sitting there having dinner, I watch and laugh at him in my head.

Today I jumped up there, and the table was nice and cool, so I stretched out, thinking it would be a good place for a nap. The Woman walked in, stopped and looked at me, and asked, "What do you think you're doing?"

Well, duh.
Getting ready to fall asleep, obviously.

Then in her infinite wisdom she pointed out, "You're getting cat germs all over the table."

Well. Yeah. That's kind of the point.
But she didn't make me get off!
She just turned around and went back to her office!

I think maybe she saw my butt hanging over the place where the Man eats, and decided to just let me rub my feline wonder all over it.

JANUARY 4, 2004

Okay. Most of the time I appreciate the fact that I don't have to clean out my own litter box. And I understand that by the very nature of using it, some litter is going to get on the floor, and the Woman finds that unpleasant. But come on...she should not deposit back into the box litter that she has swept up from the floor. That's just wrong. After it's been on the floor it's contaminated or something. I certainly don't want it back in my box.

So that's why, after she swept the bathroom today, I went in and kicked it all back out, plus a little extra for good measure.

She will be so happy.

JANUARY 5, 2004

Fun game. Sit on your Person's lap, looking right at them.
Yawn.
Pretty soon, they will yawn, too.
Yawn again.
They will, too.
Lather, rinse, repeat.

JANUARY 6, 2004

White clothes.
Fresh from the dryer.
'Nuff said.

JANUARY 7, 2004

When your tummy is growling to no end and you're so hungry you think you're going to turn inside out and consume yourself, and the People keep saying it's not freaking time yet…resort to cuteness. Sometimes there's no other way.

The Woman was sitting in the office typing her fingers off, blowing me off every time I brought up the subject of food, so I jumped into her lap, stood on my back legs, and wrapped my front paws around her neck. My first thought was that I could get her out of that chair real quick if I bit down on her neck, but I thought better of it when I realized I could be flung all the way across the room.

And then there was the little matter of her being too pissed off to feed me. Normally I don't care if she's pissed off, but I *was* awfully hungry.

So I do this ultimate cuteness thing, and she sighed real hard and said, "Yeah, it's ten minutes early, but I'll feed you anyway."

She is so totally my bitch, and she doesn't even realize it.

JANUARY 8, 2004

I've been pondering this for a few days:

I did something wrong, evidently, but I don't know what it is. It must have been huge, because they took my tree away. Worse, I sat there and watched the Woman remove all the shiny, dangly things, and then the Man literally ripped the tree apart, limb by limb. It was horrific, and I'm sure I'll have nightmares about it for the rest of my life.

No one else seemed concerned. The younger humans didn't seem bothered by the destruction of my tree, not at all. I'm the only one who seems to care, so whatever wrath they were visiting on the house must have been aimed directly at me.

The people are confusing anyway. There was the shrimp: first I didn't get any, then I did. Then they left a little in the sink and when I jumped up there to get it, they shoo'd me away. Then later when they had more, I got some, but just a little. They had all these boxes on the floor for me to play in, and then they took those away, too.

It would help if I knew what the heck I've been doing wrong.

JANUARY 9, 2004

Disturbing my routine is not acceptable.

We should all have it memorized by now: get your butt out of bed no later than 8:00 a.m., feed me, make the bed so that I have the fuzzy blanket upon which to nap, leave me alone, make a lap for me at noon, don't move while I nap, take 2 minutes to use the giant litter box while I munch on some dry food at 3 p.m., make another lap for me and don't move while I nap, get up off your ass at 5 p.m. to feed me again, fix your own dinner at 6 p.m. and make sure it's something I will also enjoy, get on your computer after dinner but make sure you leave me lap space so that I can nap, then go to bed at 11 p.m. and leave me the hell alone. I will serenade you at 3 a.m.

Got that?

Staying up *all night long* is simply unacceptable. It throws me off balance, keeps me awake, disturbs my sense of the time, and I totally forget to sing at 3 a.m. And the noise! Holy crap, when you people stay up all night, you're obnoxiously loud. Go to bed, dammit! And especially don't stay up all night long and then *leave* without feeding me!

Imbeciles.

JANUARY 10, 2003

That bird in the air, it's a blimp.
That guy over there, he's a wimp.
It's just my bad luck
That my poetry does suck
But get over it, and give me some shrimp.

JANUARY 11, 2004

They're gone.

The Younger Human and his Much Better Smelling Friend are gone. I noticed a conspicuous absence yesterday—it was very quiet—so today I explored the house, in particular the room they were in, and all their stuff is gone.

He left me again.

I tried to tell the Man this morning, and then the Woman later, but they either don't believe me, or they don't care. Or maybe it's *their fault* that they left. That must be it. They just drove the Younger Ones away.

I think I might be scarred for life.
And this time I really mean it.

JANUARY 12, 2004

Yeah, I can see that you got your hair cut.
No, I don't think it looks good.
So…?

JANUARY 13, 2004

Know what?

If a person is bending over at the same time a cat is jumping up, there will be sore heads all around.

At least the person can take an aspirin or something.

JANUARY 14, 2003

Something in the kitchen smelled good.

So, being somewhat curious, I decided to find out what it was. I jumped up on the counter and looked around, but I didn't see anything obvious. So I started sniffing around. Sniffing is a good way to track down appealing odors, and sooner or later I tend to find whatever it is I'm looking for.

This smell seemed to be coming from the sink, so I carefully put my forepaws in the sink and sniffed further. It smelled like chicken, really *good* chicken, and it was down this hole in the sink.

Here's a hint, people. When a cat is sniffing in the sink, *don't* sneak up and shout "Get your head out of the garbage disposal!"

It's not my fault you put some perfectly good chicken down there. How else will I get it if I don't stick my head down there?

Like, what could possibly go wrong?

JANUARY 15, 2004

You will not believe what they did to me today.
She held me down, and he stuck this *thing* in my mouth, and rubbed it all over my teeth!
And he did it for a *long* time!

JANUARY 16, 2004

*They did it **again!***

I was comfy and cozy on the Woman's lap, and he walked up to me with that evil stick-like thing, shoved it in my mouth, and rubbed it all over my teeth again.

That the hell did I ever do to them?

On the plus side, I've discovered a new and valuable use for the otherwise useless humans. In a spasm of itchies, the Woman demonstrated a wonderful talent of using her pitiful people-type claws to reach the major itch-fit working its way down my back. My spine was on fire, and she quite effectively put an end to it. She was very patient, too—I think she spent a good 15 minutes scratching my back and under my collar.

Something else good about them, aside from their opposable thumbs.

JANUARY 17, 2004

How can you possibly run out of kitty treats?
How?
HOW???

JANUARY 18, 2004

Not to get all Chicken Little on your collective asses, but the freaking sky really *was* falling today! I shit you not! I was sitting on my window perch, and it started to fall down, these huge, white, fluffy pieces that came down almost slowly. At first I thought it was some strange mass of bugs, but no...I looked up and it was the *sky*.

And my people? Hells Bells, they were sitting there at the table playing some stupid game and I tried to warn them about it, but did they care? The Woman looked up and *laughed at me*, saying that there was nothing she could do about it.

Well, Lady, I tell you what. Next time it happens *close the freaking window!* Give us at least a little protection!

Sheesh.

JANUARY 19, 2004

Something to ponder: why do people want to pet cats so much? Do you people not realize you have your own fur-type stuff on the top of your head, and you could easily stroke that instead? Let us kitties sleep, and pet your own self!

JANUARY 20, 2004

Ohhhhh. I've discovered something nice. Very nice.

In the room with the Peoples' oddly shaped litter box, there's this thing coming out of the wall near the floor. It's not very attractive, but it blows warm air. And not just a little here and there, but most of the time! I can lay there and it's like laying in a perfectly formed, never moving spot of sunshine.

Once in a while the air stops, but the spot stays warm, and if I wait a few minutes, it blows again.

It crossed my mind that maybe they put it there just for me, but then I realized that no, they wouldn't do that. They put it there for them, to keep themselves warm while sitting on that weird litter box thingy. I've decided that's fine, as long as it's there, and as long as they don't mind me hogging it when no one else is in there.

You know, the Woman is always cold. I wonder why she doesn't get on the floor and curl up in front of it?

JANUARY 21, 2004

My People are obsessed with my teeth. Perhaps because the lovely PK—a feline who owns a friend of theirs—lost a few of hers, or perhaps because they merely like to torture me, but in the end, it's an obsession, and it involves my mouth.

Look, I don't care for having things shoved in my mouth. Not even the good things, like shrimp or sharp cheddar cheese. If it's something I want, I'm perfectly capable of getting it from wherever it is into my own mouth, thank you very much. So I don't understand why they feel compelled to hold me down and force that stick on me just about every night now.

I get the grasp of it, finally. It's the "brushing of the teeth." Supposedly, it's to keep them healthy and useful until the day I drop dead from the plaque clogging my arteries—plaque that will be there, we can be sure, from the miscellaneous treats they give me, especially the meaty ones I manage to guilt them into every once in a while.

So yeah, when I keel over at age 15 from massive heart disease, my teeth will be blindingly white, and I'll still be really pissed off that every freaking night they do that to me.

JANUARY 22, 2004

What is the point of having a tank full of fishies that will never get big enough to eat? They're not even snack worthy. Really, that's nothing but a 37 gallon tease.

JANUARY 23, 2004

:::yawn:::
=stretch=

Mission for today: take a 10 hour nap instead of just an 8 hour one.
I don't need the beauty sleep, just the challenge.

JANUARY 24, 2004

There are *more* places in the house where warm air comes out of the wall right by the floor. There's also one in the room where the Younger Humans stayed, and one in the room where the People sleep—and today the Woman took my basket with the comfy pillow from its cold spot downstairs, and brought it upstairs to put it right in front of the rushing warm air for me. Now not only do I have my perpetual spot of sunshine, but I have it plus a cushy, comfy bed in which to enjoy it.

Oh yeah, I be stylin'...

JANUARY 25, 2004

It is *so* not funny to make a loud buzzing sound and touch a kitty on the tummy when he's sound asleep and on his back. *So* not funny!

JANUARY 26, 2004

When I'm sitting atop the Supreme Commander Kitty Tower, I am not plotting to overthrow the people of the house. Honestly, that thought had never occurred to me. The only thing I'm thinking up there is how much better than them I am.

JANUARY 27, 2004

The ground outside is white, and the People don't seem to like it any more than I do. The Man was complaining about it getting all over his truck, and the Woman says it's just cold, nasty stuff that she won't drive on. Granted, I'm not terribly sure what that means, other than they agree with me. The white stuff has to go.

I thought it was, a little while ago. Most of it had disappeared overnight, but then the sky began to fall and there it was again. The Woman says it's "pretty" even though she wishes it would stop, but I think the whole thing is just nasty. And I'm pretty sure that white stuff is why it's so damned cold.

Sure, I have my warm places to lay, especially the warm spot where my bed is now, but the windows are too cold to sit next to, and I usually like sitting on my window perches, looking outside. Why bother when it makes all my useless nipples pucker? And I can feel that, you know, as they crinkle and try to invert. It's not terribly pleasant.

I'm going back to bed. Wake me when its over.

JANUARY 28, 2004

I don't do hugs
And I hate kissing
I do bite some
And I'm good at hissing.

Poetry By Max. Save it. Someday it'll be worth something.

JANUARY 29, 2004

The Woman has been drinking this stuff she calls "hot chocolate." It smells pretty good, but she won't let me get so much as a taste of it. There's all these excuses: "you'll burn your tongue. It's not cat food. Kitties can't have anything chocolate."

Just be honest with me, will you? You won't let me taste it because you just don't want to share. Don't pretend it has anything to do with trying to do what's right for me; you have something good, and you want it all for yourself.

I'm not stupid. Hey, I might not even *like* it, but I should at least get the chance to find out.

I'd let you have a taste of my food, it you asked.
Really I would.
In fact, if you go in the kitchen, you can lick my plate right now.

JANUARY 30, 2004

The sky has been falling all over the place, in huge white chunks that have pretty much covered everything outside. I've given up trying to warn the People, because they just don't seem to care about it.

Today, though, the Man went outside and scooped up a handful of the stuff, and brought it inside to show to me. Like I wasn't already a little freaked out about the whole thing! But he held it out to me, and I sniffed for a few seconds, pretending I didn't give a damn, but you know what?

The sky is freaking *cold!*

Kind of makes you wonder why the birds bother flying through it.

JANUARY 31, 2004

What do I have to do to get you to turn the freaking heat up already? I've asked the People over and over and over, but they just wander off to bed—turning it *down*—and leave me there to freeze. I've pointed out what happens to my useless nipples, but they don't care. The Woman has noticed that sometimes my fur is cold, but it's like she's too dense to get it.

I bet if they hadn't cut my nads off, and those suddenly vanished because of shrinkage they'd notice.

All I'm asking for is a little heat.
And more Stinky Goodness.

Yeah, the Stinky Goodness would be most appreciated.
If it's fresh dead live fish, I'd be happy to shiver a little longer.

FEBRUARY 1, 2004

The stuff in the glass *looked* like water. But it sure didn't taste like water. How can People drink that? It hurt my tongue…all fizzy and bubbly and whatnot. That can't be good for anyone.

FEBRUARY 2, 2004

Well this is just craptastic.

They're both in bed and sound asleep, and no one remembered to fill my dish with dry food so I'd have sustenance to get me through the night.

It's like 3 a.m. and I'm starving.

If I die before they get up, you'll know who to blame.

FEBRUARY 3, 2004

I've been watching the fishies in the tank, and the thought occurred to me: maybe they put the fish tank there for me. Those fishies are small right now, but they could grow to a decent size if the man keeps giving them that funky smelling flaky food. And if they grow to a decent size, they'll surely be snack worthy. Maybe even meal worthy if I have more than one at a time.

I don't think they'll get big enough to get really excited over, but snack worthy size would be nice. At that size, the Man wouldn't even need to pull the guts and bones out. I'd eat them whole. The crunchiness might be quite satisfying.

FEBRUARY 4, 2004

You know what's not fair? People can eat whenever they want, whatever they want. I have to freaking *ask* for food, and nine times out of ten they're so dense they don't understand what I want, which means I have to resort to begging.

They leave out this dry crap for me, but dammit, they should know what I want! I shouldn't have to humiliate myself for a can of Stinky Goodness!

I hate people.
Damn them and their opposable thumbs.

FEBRUARY 5, 2004

Here's a thought: if you don't want me to lick the chicken, don't leave it on the counter.
Simple as that.

FEBRUARY 6, 2004

If God didn't want me to head-butt you awake every morning, he would not have placed your nose so far out from your face, where it is within easy reach.

FEBRUARY 7, 2004

If I look out the back window, I can see into the house of the people behind us. They used to have two cats, and one of them kind of looked like me. They were inside cats, which is a good thing, but I would have liked to have talked to them. I think they're gone now. All I ever see in that house now is this yappy little white dog. You know, the kind that does nothing but yip and yap and shiver and pee on the floor.

Come to think of it, the people don't look the same, either.

I wonder where the cats took them...?

FEBRUARY 8, 2004

The Woman has a huge desk, and she doesn't have a whole lot on it. Just her computer, a printer, and a phone. Oh, and some assorted paperwork and there's *always* a drink can. She can't live without having a drink can within arm's length. I really think that if there's no can, she'll curl up in a big ball of human stink and cry, or just quit breathing. I think she needs those drink cans more than the average kitty needs kitty crack.

But still...

The desk is huge, and there's plenty of space for me to lounge there, behind the computer. But does she let me?

Hell no. Every stinking time I jump up there, she picks me up and sets me on the floor and says, "Not now, Max." Not now for what? It's not like she has to *do* anything while I stretch out on the back side of her desk. I'm not hurting anything.

Doesn't she realize that I could be her muse?

FEBRUARY 9, 2004

I overheard the Woman telling the Man that she ought to give me a bath. What the hell? I'm perfectly capable of giving myself a bath, and I bet I do a much better job than a Person would do!

And you know *why* she says she ought to give me a bath?

"To see what he would do."

I can already tell you, lady, and it involves things of yours meeting toothy deaths, a considerable amount of my poop on your keyboard, pillow, and shoes, as well as much screaming and crying, and many, many, many sleepless nights for you.

Oh, and I have no problem with crawling carefully up onto the bed if you *do* manage to fall asleep just to stick my tongue up your nose.

Or worse, rub my ass all over your face.

So go ahead, try it.

FEBRUARY 10, 2004

Hey. If I can see the bottom of the bowl, it's time for *someone* to refill it. Really, what kind of effort does it take to pour out a little dry food? Obviously, more than you can handle today.

FEBRUARY 11, 2004

If you see a paw sticking out from under the door, it means one of two things:

Let me out.
=or=
Let me in.

It does not mean "Let's screw with the cat and tickle his little paw," nor does it mean, "grab his little paw and see what he'll do."

He'll get mightily upset, that's what.

And no, you're not allowed to go to the bathroom without me.
No real reason why.
You're just not.

FEBRUARY 12, 2004

Oooh. You know what's fun?
A box of Kleenex, that's what.
And you know what's even more fun?
The People when they see how you've redecorated with just a single box of Kleenex.

FEBRUARY 13, 2004

It's not fair. I got to the comfy chair first, and what do you do? You pick me up and stick me on your lap. If I wanted to be on your lap, I'd climb up there myself. But I'm flexible, so I wander into the other room and curl up in the desk chair. I get nice and comfortable, and almost asleep, and what do you do?

You freaking come in there, pick me up and take me back to the other chair, so you can sit at the desk!

And you do the same damn thing at least twice more in one evening!
Make up your fricking mind!

Yeah, yeah, yeah, so you actually moved me from one chair to another nice one, when you could have just dumped me on the floor...but Lady, you could have just *let me sleep!* You only moved me 'cause you're afraid I'll leave you a present on your pillow.

FEBRUARY 14, 2004

Holy crap. People, if you leave something out on the counter, I am not responsible for what might happen to it. If I find it attractive in any way, shape, or form, I am going to at least take a closer look at it. If it's in a plastic bag…well, yes, I *do* have to rip it to shreds. And if what's inside is edible, I have to taste it. And if it's too big to chew, I have to rip it to shreds. And yes, I am going to leave everything there for you to clean up.

FEBRUARY 15, 2004

No, I don't care if you don't want me on top of the TV. It's warm, and I want to nap there. Live with it.

FEBRUARY 16, 2004

See? See what happens when you let Sticky Little People touch you?
NOTHING GOOD, that's for sure!
I could have told them that, but they never listen, anyway.

The Man let Sticky Little People touch him, and now he's sick. He's got this nasty cough and he keeps blowing his nose like it's some sort of magical horn, and he sounds like he ate a blowtorch.

All this from letting one of THOSE creatures get too close.

I'm telling you, People, you need to get rid of the little ones. They're dangerous things to have around.

FEBRUARY 17, 2004

Strange fishy, found while sneakily poking through the Woman's hard drive:

I think I'm glad this never winds up in one of my cans of Stinky Goodness. That skin looks awfully hard to chew through...

FEBRUARY 18, 2004

No, my ass is not on fire.
Can't a cat run around the house without a lot of questions?

FEBRUARY 19, 2004

If you don't like waking up with my ass in your face, may I suggest that you get your lazy self up about an hour earlier than you normally do? It would benefit both of us: I would get fed when I'm hungry, and you'd avoid the glory of the remnants of things YOU had cut off WITHOUT my consent.

FEBRUARY 20, 2004

Hmmm.
Yes.
I *am* rather proud of the 7 pound poop I left in the litter box.
Pride is why I didn't bury it.
You should be honored that I wanted to share it with you.

FEBRUARY 21, 2004

All right. If they look like balls, and roll like balls, I should be able to play with them.

Right?

So don't get your shorts in a wad if you leave ball-like objects where I can reach them, and don't yell at me for playing with the eggs.

The way I see it, the issue is that you're denying me my toys, not that I'm playing with your food.

FEBRUARY 22, 2004

Let's get something straight:

If it's on the floor, it's mine.
If you drop it, it's mine.
If it's on the table and you walk away from it, it's mine.
If it's on the counter and you're not looking, it's mine.
In fact, if it's in your hand and I can get to it, it's mine.

Got it?
Good.

February 23, 2004

So I climbed into the dishwasher. What's the big deal? The dishes were clean, so I didn't lick them or anything. I just wanted to see what was inside…the Woman picked me up and deposited me to the floor in a fairly rough manner, and told me the dishwasher is no place for a kitty to play.

Well, duh. I wasn't playing, I was just looking. Since when is just looking a crime?

Really, some people need to lighten up a bit, and pick the wad out of their shorts.

February 24, 2004

Apparently, I don't show my appreciation for the things my People do for me. The Woman says so, therefore it must be true.

Yeah.
Well.

If they're really nice to me today, feed me on time, don't touch my belly, give me fresh water, and feed me some more, I'll give popping out a nice heart shaped poop a good try.

Show 'em the love. Yep.

February 25, 2004

The Sticky Little Creatures are back; at least, they're outside more often, yelling and screaming and laughing at these horrible, ear-splitting levels. I sit in my window and watch them—heck, even the birds scatter when one of them gets close. Who can blame them?

The other day the Woman left the front door open, and took the glass off the screen so we could get some fresh air, and the Man put a box in front of it so I could see out better. They went outside, I think to talk to other People (though I haven't figured out why that's so much fun, just sitting there and talking without food being involved), but after a while he brought one of the Sticky Little Creatures to the door to see me.

I don't mind this one so much, as long as he stays on that side of the door. He doesn't squeal at me, and even if I press my face up to the screen, he doesn't poke. There's some kind of game he was trying to play—he kept crouching down where I couldn't see him and then he popped back up—but I didn't get it. It amused him, so what the heck.

The key is that door…as long as the Sticky Things stay on the outside, I can tolerate them, I suppose. They are entertaining sometimes, especially when they're rolling down the street on their wheeled toys, and sometimes even when they get seriously ticked off at the Big People.

I love a good temper tantrum.

It's nice out today, but I haven't seen any of them out there yet. I think the Big People are hiding them.

FEBRUARY 26, 2004

Look, I don't know what your last nerve is, but if I'm on it, I don't care.

I don't know what Professional Wrestling is, nor who Hulk Hogan and Steve Austin are. I don't care.

But if a "body slam" gets your lazy ass out of bed in the morning to feed me, I'm going to keep doing it.

If you would get up a couple hours earlier, and feed me *before* you head for the giant litter box and *before* you get dressed, I wouldn't have to do it. So until then, enjoy the 14 pounds of slick, black, furry feline wonder dropping onto your gut, baby.

FEBRUARY 27, 2004

Newsflash:

It is *not* funny to lift the lid on the giant litter box when you see me running into the bathroom to spend a little quality time with you.

There's *water* in there!

FEBRUARY 28, 2004

Enough with the stupid laser pointer!
I *know* where the red dot is coming from, and I'm not chasing it anymore!

MARCH 1, 2004

That thing on your desk is *not* a mouse.
I swear.

MARCH 2, 2004

Last night the People cooked their food out in the back yard—don't ask me why, that's just asking for the birds to poop on it—and it smelled really good. I mean *really* good. But did I get any, even after being very good and patient while they ate? Hell no. All I got was this lame explanation for not sharing: "I don't think kitties can have pork."

I don't know what "pork" is, but it smelled good enough for me to eat, so why not at least let me *try* it? You let me eat fish and chicken and turkey, why not pork??? They're all dead things, aren't they?

On the plus side, the Man did give me treats early in the morning. He felt bad because he kicked me in the ass while trying to walk through the dark. He *could* have turned a light on, but no…he just wanders through the dark, waiting for cat ass to pummel with that giant foot.

It all worked out. He gave me food, so I wasn't starving ten minutes after he left the house, and I didn't have to wake the Woman before she was ready to get up. She was happy, and even came downstairs to feed me the good stuff before she went upstairs to shower.

Still…I wanted that pork last night. And since I didn't get it, I had to head-butt her awake this morning.

That's only fair.

MARCH 3, 2004

If you have a donut, you're required (by law, I think) to share it with me.
It doesn't matter if it's not good for a kitty.
It doesn't even matter if I don't actually eat the piece you give me.
It doesn't matter if all I do is lick it.
YOU HAVE TO SHARE!!!

MARCH 4, 2004

There's a reason kitties always have to sit on your lap or rub against your legs when you're wearing black pants.

I didn't say I'd share the reason, I just thought I should point out that there *is* a reason.

It involves pissing you off and amusing us.

MARCH 5, 2004

There once was a cat who was white
He was outside and got in a fight
He rolled in the mud
Which hid all the blood
He then got a bath, that's not right.

Even more poetry by Max.

MARCH 6, 2004

From my email:

Why do you seem irritated so much of the time?

Because I have to deal with Humans, that's why.
Ask a stupid question…

MARCH 7, 2004

You know it's a strong wind when the birds are getting up-ended onto their feathery little asses. Makes me very glad I can sit here inside, where it's nice and warm, looking out the window, laughing at them.

MARCH 8, 2004

No, I do not know what happened to the kitty crack toy you gave me just 2 days ago. No, I do not care to go looking for it. Just give me another one, and we'll both be happy.

MARCH 9, 2004

Why the hell does the Woman call me "Hoover" or "Eureka" when I'm eating???

MARCH 10, 2004

See? See what I have to do to get warm enough to take a nap?

TURN UP THE HEAT!
My nipples are inverting...

~ ~ ~

Okay. For the last week or so, the Man has gotten up at a reasonable hour to feed me. I've enjoyed it, to be honest, getting fed before my stomach is rumbling so loud it wakes the birds outside.

This morning he got up especially early and *left*. He went back to work! So right around the time I was getting hungry, the only Human left in the house was still asleep. I was not happy. Not at all. It was nice to not have to work to get someone up and get them downstairs, and I would have appreciated notice that I was going to have to fall back on old routines in order to get the food out of the freaking can and onto the plate.

I was nice, I didn't head butt her, not until I heard the birds outside, mocking me. And when that didn't work, I crawled onto her chest and stuck my nose up hers. And when *that* didn't work, I knocked her glasses off the night stand.

Let me tell you, she hates that. But it works. She gets all pissy on me and makes me get off the bed, but she gets up. Usually the getting up is accompanied by all this muttering and swearing, and threats of locking me in a bathroom, but she doesn't mean it. After all, if she were *really* mad, she wouldn't get up. She'd toss me across the room, and she hasn't done that.

Yet.

MARCH 11, 2004

For whatever reason (hell, even I'm not sure) I jumped into the tub today while the Woman was getting dressed, and she said, "You know, my sister used to have a cat who pooped in the tub. I am *so* glad you don't do that."

Well…now that the idea has been put into my head…

MARCH 12, 2004

Oh, yeah, like you're *really* going to beat my little ass for biting your nose while you were still in bed this morning.

First, you can't catch me.
Second, you've *never* hit me and I doubt you'll start now.
Third…well, I know an empty threat when I hear one.

Besides, it's not like I chomped down. I just wanted you to know I was there, and starving to death.

Look, no matter what she says, I did *not* lay across the Woman's face this morning.

I was merely stepping over her head, and stumbled.

Any resemblance to laying across her face is coincidental.

MARCH 14, 2004

Not that I'm nosy or anything, but I overheard the Woman talking to that thing she holds to her ear tonight, and she was talking about me.

Now, over time I've come to the conclusion that somewhere there's another Human with another thing held to the ear, and they can hear each other. It just makes sense, in an odd sort of way. Why she can't just talk to the Man, or even me, instead of someone with another thing pressed against the ear escapes me, but what the hell. They don't consult me in matters of logic.

Anyway.

She was talking about me. And *laughing*. Making fun of how I approach my water dish. As if there's something abnormal about it.

Look, no matter what she says I don't actually *stalk* my water. Yeah, sure, sometimes when I'm across the room I crouch down and watch it carefully, and yeah, sure, sometimes my butt wiggles, and yeah, sure sometimes after that I race across the room towards it. But I'm not *stalking* it. I'm just making sure that there's no one else around it.

Besides, for all you know there is a good reason to attack the water dish. For all you People can know, there's *things* near the dish that have to be dispelled before I can safely take a drink. Remember, I have much better eyesight than you People do. I have a better sense of smell, too, and let's just say some of you need to lick yourself more thoroughly.

And even if I did stalk my water dish, that's not really the point. The point is that it's *rude* to talk about a cat behind his back, especially if you're laughing at him. I have good hearing, too. Want me to tell the world what kinds of sounds I hear emanating from *you* when you think no one else is around?

I also heard the Woman saying she was going to pick me up and squeeze me. She so is *not* going to do that. I may not have my claws anymore, but I still have teeth. People would do well to remember that.

MARCH 15, 2004

There is absolutely no need to comment on the size of my tummy. So it flops back and forth when I run... Take a look at the average lion. *He* has a flopping back and forth tummy, too. It's a feline guy thing.

Besides, have *you* taken a look in the mirror lately?

MARCH 16, 2004

=^. .^=

Look.
Kitty art.

MARCH 17, 2004

I didn't feel so hot when I got up this morning, but I made the Woman get up to feed me anyway.

And even though my tummy hurt a bit, I ate the food she gave me.

The end result was that I puked it up, but my aim was really good—I made sure I made it to a place on the floor where there's carpet instead of linoleum. I don't think she appreciated my efforts, though. And she's gagging like crazy while she tries to clean it up, so much so that I think she'll puke, too.

I feel better already.

MARCH 18, 2004

Want to make yourself nauseous?

Plop down on a bed, on your back, and look up at the ceiling fan. Pick a spot on one of the blades, and watch it go round and round and round.

Yep, that'll do it.

MARCH 19, 2004

One of the things I have fun with most mornings is knocking the Woman's glasses off the nightstand. It's not that I want to play with them, but she hates it, and that amuses me.

I also like crawling onto her lap, and stretching up like I'm going to give her a kitty kiss. If I time it just right, I can smear my nose across her glasses while they're on her face, and she *really* hates that. And that amuses me.

But lately, she's not wearing them. Most of the time they're next to the bathroom sink, where it's not nearly as much fun to whack at them or drag my nose across them. Come to think of it, the Man isn't wearing his either, not at all. If he lost them, he's going to be in a lot of trouble. And I want to be there when he is. That will amuse me, too.

It's just not as much fun trying to run boogers onto the Woman's face without those glasses—she usually stops me. And that doesn't amuse me one bit.

MARCH 20, 2004

Ok.
No matter what she claims, I did *not* stick my tongue up the Woman's nose this afternoon.
Not intentionally, anyway.

MARCH 21, 2004

Wow. Did you know that if you surf around online, all the websites that have names that sound like they should be run by cats *aren't*? And People, how *do* you contort yourselves into positions like that? And more importantly...*why*?

MARCH 22, 2004

Why do people email me with strange and pointless offers? I don't need a genuine Replica Ro.Lex watch, I don't need bigger boobs, and a bigger penis is pointless since the People had the goodies that go along with that cut off. I don't have a bank account, so I can't give you the number so that you can deposit the wealth of all of Nigeria into it. Do you people not know you're sending those offers to a cat?

If you're going to offer me something, how about a credit card? I could really use one of those, you know. There's some neat stuff online for a cat to buy...

MARCH 23, 2004

After the Woman washes her hair, I sometimes like to stick my face against her head and rub my nose in her hair, sometimes taking a nibble or two. There's something oddly appealing about her hair when it's wet, and it gets me a little bit high.

Kind of like kitty crack.

But today. Oh my God. She washed her hair and I jumped up on the back of the sofa to take a deep breath (and perhaps a tiny mouthful), and the smell… Holy guacamole, that was awful! My eyes started to water it was so bad.

I jumped down and glared at her, but all she did was laugh and say, "Mentholated shampoo, Furball."

Whatever.
That stuff should be illegal.

MARCH 24, 2004

Ahhhhh
Know what's really nice? When the People take a load of towels out of the dryer, dump it on the love seat, and don't get mad when you curl up in the pile.
Soooooo nice…

MARCH 25, 2004

Want to see the Woman really grumpy?

Just be here first thing in the morning on a day when she looks into the fridge and realizes she's out of cans full of the bubbly water.

You will learn new and colorful words, let me tell you…

MARCH 27, 2004

Things that make you go "Hmmmm…"
Or maybe, "What the F—?"

My people do (don't tell them I said so) buy me good quality food. They spend the money on the really good Stinky Goodness that I enjoy so much (Fancy Feast for those wondering) and a tasty lower-calorie dry food upon which I can nosh pretty much at will. The thing is, not only do they get me stuff I like, they make sure it's good for me.

So.
Why do people not do that for themselves?
Why do people seem to enjoy eating so much *crap?*

My People are no different. They have a fondness for cookies in particular, it seems, and I've heard the Woman say they shouldn't eat them because they have so many calories, and calories make people fat. She especially likes the bubbly water, and while she says that has no calories, it's probably not good for her teeth.

Well now.
Even I know a Person needs their teeth, just like a kitty does.

How can one rip through real live cooked dead meat without a set of especially fine teeth? And I know people like that stuff; they're fairly adept at cooking it up (and sometimes sharing…) and they enjoy it from time to time. Why risk the teeth when you need them for gnawing on the *really* good stuff?

I don't knock peoples' priorities, not when it comes to feeding their pets. We *do* make their lives bearable, after all. But people…if you don't eat the right foods, you might not be as healthy as your kitties and puppies, and you might die. And if you die, who will open our cans of Stinky Goodness?

Hmmm?

MARCH 28, 2004

Lady, don't complain so much when I get you up in the morning.

Just think about how your life would be without me.

You'd sleep too late every day, you'd come home to an empty house every time you've gone out, you'd have no company while you sit on the giant litter box in the bathroom, you'd be lonely while you're typing away on the computer, and your clothes wouldn't keep you nearly as warm without the layer of fur I generously deposit upon them.

You need me, and you know it.

MARCH 29, 2004

The People bought me some tasty new dry food about a week ago. Not that I'll admit it to them (because then the perfect wet Stinky Goodness might disappear), but I like it. It does a much better job of making my tummy feel full, so I don't feel like I have to launch the Woman out of bed in the morning. I'm being very patient, letting her sleep until she wakes up on her own, just curled up on her tummy.

She doesn't sleep as late as I figured she would, and she's *much* nicer when I don't do a body slam into the middle of her stomach or stick something up her nose. She wakes up, stretches, tells me I'm a good kitty and scratches behind my ears and under my collar (ohmygod, that is too good…but I won't tell her how much I like that), and gets up.

Now, granted, once in a while I'm still going to stick my nose up hers, or send her glasses flying across the room, but that's just for fun. And I think it's in my contract somewhere. You know, the primary Kitty Rule: Thou Shalt Be An Occasional PITA. Something I'm very good at.

Strange thing, though. It's not cold anymore; all the white stuff is gone and the birds and Sticky Little People are outside in droves, but she still shivers, keeps the heat up, and curls up under the bright red and blue blanket. She swears she's cold, but I think she's just looking for sympathy. And for me to curl up in her lap. Selfish thing.

MARCH 30, 2004

If you don't want me to play in the room with the loud boxes that get your clothes all wet, then you should keep the door closed.

Granted, it would be nice if you would, just once, leave both the door *and* the opening to one of those boxes open, just so I could peek inside. I won't barf or poop in them, I promise.

It stinks in that room, too. You should clean it sometimes.

MARCH 31, 2004

What makes you think I would chase a mouse? Even a fake one?
Do you *ever* see cans of Stinky Goodness with a "Mouse Inside" label?
If Fancy Feast doesn't make it, I won't eat it.
And if I won't eat it, why would I chase it?

Bugs don't count.
Those I can torture without hearing their little screams of terror.

APRIL 1, 2004

I discovered something new and annoying this morning.
When the People won't get up, stick your cold, wet nose up against one of their closed eyelids.
You'll wind up being bounced onto the bed, but it's worth it.

APRIL 2, 2004

I think they're mad at me again, but I don't know why. The Man came home and chased me around the house with that horrible stick he rubs all over my teeth, and he managed to corner me on my window perch and did it while all the birds outside could see. And they were mocking me, I know they were! I could hear them chirping away, laughing at the poor bastard feline being molested by the much larger human.

Then the Woman comes home and she has this thing in a shiny purple bag, and on the bag are these bright ribbony things. It was pretty, and I wanted to see what was in it. But would she let me stick my head in the bag to see? Hell, no. First she chased me off the table, and when I went back (thinking she wasn't looking) she caught me and then took the shiny purple bag and hid it in the pantry, where I can't get to it.

I just want to see what's in the bag! But nooooo, it's "not for the kitty." It's "a present for someone else."

When do *I* get a present?

~ ~ ~

I almost always take a nap after the People have their dinner. Always. Almost. They eat, and if I act cute or quiet and don't beg, I usually get a tiny bite, and then I go jump on the big fuzzy blanket on the big bed and go to sleep for a while.

So what happens tonight? The Woman finishes eating and while the Man is getting me a bite, *she* goes and lies down in the spot where I was going to nap! Right smack dab in the middle of the bed! The *good* part!

I jumped up there anyway and jammed my butt up against her, hoping to shove her aside just enough to get the sweet spot. She moved a little bit, but dammit, then she reached out and pulled me close to her. To *snuggle*.

I swear, if she hadn't felt so toasty warm, I would have turned around and bit her.
Hard.
I mean it.

APRIL 3, 2004

What is *wrong* with these People? They run around the house, going in and out, leaving me alone most of the day with only dry food and filtered water to subsist on, and when they come home, what do they do?

They open a door, so of course I have to investigate, and once I go through, they shut the freaking door! *She locked me in the frigging closet again!*

Really, once is a mistake. Twice is a sign of senility. But this—this *has* to be intentional. She said she was sorry, but she was laughing when she said it, so I don't think so.

Yeah, lady, if you're reading this, what I'm thinking rhymes with "witch."

APRIL 4, 2004

The Woman was out ~~getting drunk~~ shopping—I'm sure of that because she brought bags home—but did she buy me anything?

Phffft.

I am in need of some fresh kitty crack.
She *knows* that.

APRIL 5, 2004

I saw shrimp!
I did, I did, I did see shrimp!

The Woman was unloading bags of food, and I saw her put a big thing of shrimp in the freezer. Like 30 or 40 of them.

But *in the freezer*!!!

Do they want me to break my teeth?
I'll eat them, sure, but it might not be pretty.

APRIL 6, 2004

Peoples.
Change my litter box.
Now.
Or you know what will happen.

APRIL 7, 2004

Yes, you do look fat in that.

APRIL 8, 2004

Oh man, I hit the Trifecta of Pissing The Woman Off this morning. I didn't start too early—I waited until her normal time to get up, but she was being pretty lazy about getting up, so I didn't have a whole lot of choice.

I started off with a fairly gentle body slam into her stomach, but all that did was make her grunt and push me aside, then roll over. I waited, hoping she would sit up, but she didn't, she just went right back to sleep.

So, I had to up the ante, so to speak. I carefully crawled up the bed, onto her pillow, and dropped like a dead weight onto her head. That got me a "Dammit, stop it," but she still didn't get up.

I had no choice.

I went for the glasses.

I sent those suckers flying, and she knew it. She reached out and grabbed me, tossing me across the bed, but she *still* didn't get up. Every time I tried to climb over her, she shoved me away. Like I would give up.

Eventually she did finally get up, and boy was she mad. She was down on her hands and knees looking for her glasses, saying words that I know I'm too young to hear. Even a threat: "I'm not f$@#ing feeding you right now, you little shit."

Yeah right.

She found the glasses, went to the giant litter box, got dressed, and what did she do?

She fed me.

I win.

APRIL 9, 2004

I've got the Woman right where I want her, and she doesn't even know it. Like this afternoon—I was hungry and let her know it, but she just scratched my head and said "I'm not feeding you. It's only four o'clock and you have to wait until five."

Not good enough.

I meowed and crawled all over her lap, stretched up and nibbled at her hair, got in her face—I was not going to give up, not until she was frustrated enough to just get up and give me the second half of my can of Stinky Goodness.

And it worked!

It only took an hour, but she finally got tired of it, and get up to feed me.

So there.

APRIL 10, 2004

More Kitty Fun:

Stand on the back of the sofa, as close to one of your Humans as is felinely possible. When they take a drink of bubbly water, really fast lean over and stick your tongue in their ear.

The bubbly water will shoot out their nose.

It's funny as hell, I swear.

APRIL 11, 2004

Happy Easter my ass. You know how I celebrated? Do you?

It started out with the Woman, in all her glorious stupidity, locking me in the closet *again!* She opened it to get some clothes out, and you'd think by now she'd *know* that I like to go in and curl up on the blanket in there. But nooooo…she closed the freaking door and it took *two hours* before she realized I was in there.

To make matters worse, the People disappeared for most of the day, and she was late in getting my dinner. Oh, she said she was sorry, but I don't believe it. No way. She ran in the front door, saying how sorry she was, and she fed me, but then she turned around and left again for at least another hour.

After they came home to stay, she was in the kitchen puttering around, and I went in there to munch on the mostly-acceptable dry food, and what happens? *She stepped on me!* This wasn't a little pinch to my tail—she stomped on my entire foot with *her* entire foot. Like, about a ton of Stomping Human Femaleness. Yeah, well, I hollered a good one—because that makes her feel bad—and ran upstairs. The Man followed me up and picked me up. As if I wasn't pissed off enough, he picked me up and took me back into the freaking kitchen.

All right, he took me back so that the Woman could give me a treat or two or fifteen, but still.

These People never learn. Never.

APRIL 12, 2004

What possible reason would the People have for feeding the squirrels? Those things don't appreciate fine food. They'll eat garbage, for Pete's Sake.

Ok, so would I *if* the garbage was fish that they'd thrown out, or beef scraps, or even chicken guts, but they're leaving out corn, and the dumb thing is eating it. It's not even good corn—it's this rock hard, chew-til-your-teeth-break stuff, still on the cob.

Even I know it's probably not a good thing to eat corn that stale.

But they feed the squirrels, anyway, and then the birds come along and pick at what's left...and then the People get upset that the birds are pooping all over their cars.

Folks, if it goes in, eventually it's gonna come out the other end. And if your car just happens to be in the way...well, that's your own damn fault, isn't it?

APRIL 14, 2004

Okay, so you opened the window for me.
Big freaking deal.
Okay, so I sat there for half an hour pawing at the blinds.
That doesn't mean I wanted to sit there and stare outside.
It only meant that I wanted the blinds open.

Now they are.
Now I can go into another room.
So, there.

APRIL 15, 2004

You left the laundry basket filled with clean clothes in the living room. You know that I'm going to curl up on the clean clothes. So it's your fault that there's cat barf on your favorite sweatshirt, not mine.

~ ~ ~

You know, when I was standing on the Woman's lap this evening, trying to decide if I wanted to plop down or just annoy her, I really didn't intend to cut loose a mighty fart with my tail end towards her face.

Really, I didn't.

It was just a bonus.

APRIL 16, 2004

The Woman went somewhere today, and said she was "driving around top-less."
I hope that doesn't mean what it sounds like.
I've seen her topless.
That would just be…wrong.

APRIL 17, 2004

Don't ask me to do something cute just because you're bored. I can just per-form on demand, you know! If that's what you want, get another dog. Just don't let it in the house.

APRIL 18, 2004

I am so ashamed. I let one of the Sticky Little People touch me last night. Even worse, I let the Woman pick me up and take me outside so that the Sticky Person could do just that. I don't know why I allowed this to happen; it's just that the People were outside with the Other People all afternoon and evening, and I was in here all alone…It wasn't too bad, though. The Sticky One didn't shriek at me or tug or poke, she just touched a finger to my fur. And she tried to say my name, though it sounds more like "Math" than "Max."

No, I am not getting soft. It was just a momentary lapse in judgment.

APRIL 19, 2004

You should realize, if I don't come running when you call out my name, re-placing it with "Here, kitty, kitty" isn't going to be any more successful.

I'll come when I feel like it.

APRIL 20, 2004

Sheesh. I was stretched out on the big fuzzy blanket, and the Woman just plopped herself down, turned on the TV, and disturbed my most important evening nap. Worse yet, after a couple of minutes she reached across the bed and grabbed me, dragging me across the blanket, so she could "cuddle" and "pet me."

Holy crap. If I hadn't been just a tiny bit cold, and if I hadn't had this little itch under my chin, I would have bit her and then stomped off in a giant furry huff.

She spent FORTY FIVE minutes abusing me.
Next time, I'm biting, I swear.

Well…unless I'm cold.
Or itchy.

APRIL 21, 2004

People…no one asked you to think. Your jobs are to earn money to pay for my food, feed me—on demand—and feed me well, make the bed every morning I have a good napping place, open windows when desired, and keep the litter box clean.

This requires little to no thinking on your part.

So don't come home and tell me, "I don't think it's time for you to eat."
It is too time, if I say it is.
Stop thinking before one of us (you) gets hurt.

APRIL 22, 2004

Someone needs to notify me when my daily routine is going to be interrupted. I have things I'm used to: the Man gets up early, ignores me, reads the papers, and then leaves. I wait a while, then go upstairs and start *gently* trying to get the Woman to wake up. She eventually opens her eyes, says a bunch of bad words, gets up, uses the giant litter box, and then goes downstairs to feed me. As it should be.

So when the Man does not get up early, it worries me. What if he's late to where ever it is he goes most days? What if his not being there means they can't buy me more cans of Stinky Goodness? There are a lot of "what-ifs" involved, so I make the effort to wake him up. Or wake her up, so she can get him up. It's simply pure consideration on my part.

Do they even understand this?

Phffft. I do my best and what I get in return is "Stop it, Max. Shut up, Max.

I'm going to wrap your tail around your neck and *make* you be quiet, Max."
(Ok, honestly, no one has ever said that, but I'm pretty sure they're thinking
it.)

I swear, if they didn't have those opposable thumbs, I'd let them rot their lives
away in bed.

APRIL 23, 2004

It must be something to do with the changing of the weather from cold to
almost warm. I can't think of any other reason for there to be so many new
Sticky Little People running and crawling around outside. No matter what
window I look out, there they are, going off at full tilt, making far too much
noise for respectable creatures. One can only hope that with time, they slow
down and learn to be quieter.

Though it is kind of neat when one of the new ones learns to say my name.
Not that I pay any attention to that kind of thing.

APRIL 24, 2004

I am not grunting.

I am clearing my throat to get your attention. It's dinner time, and you don't
seem to notice.

APRIL 25, 2004

Oh, man, I saw the most amazing thing! Under the kitchen sink there are
about 50 cans of Stinky Goodness! Seriously! About *fifty* cans!

My birthday must be coming up and we must be having a party.
Or I get to have a Stinky Goodness orgy all by myself.

I vote for the latter.
Fifty cans.
Oh wow.

April 26, 2004

No matter what it looks like, I was *not* stuck up here.

I could have gotten down any time I wanted.

Really.

Oh, bite me.

April 27, 2004

The Woman had music playing today, and there was some guy singing about how it was three a.m. and he was lonely.

I know how that feels.

By three a.m., I'm pretty well rested, and it would be nice if *someone* else was up. But no...being worthless and weak, my People sleep for *hours* at time. Like 8 or 9 without taking a break (well, the Man takes breaks to pee, but that doesn't count since all he'll do is grunt at me, and then he goes right back to bed.)

I understand sleeping a good 16 hours a day, but not all at once.
And not when the cat needs company.
And food.

Especially not when the cat needs food.

APRIL 28, 2004

What's a cream puff, and why does the Woman think I'm one?

APRIL 29, 2004

Vacuums.

Yes, I think they should be illegal. I mean, come on! Those things make other things just vanish! I've seen it too many times to trust those noisy suckers. Some perfectly good crumbs that I might have been saving for *days* are right there on the floor where I want them, and along comes that vacuum and =whoosh= my crunchy stash is gone. Forever.

Everything in its path meets a sucky death. So why should I trust one? If I'm not vigilant enough and it manages to creep up behind me, I could wind up inside its filthy little belly. So yeah, those things should be against the law.

Anything that eats everything in its path should be taken outside, shot, and then enacted into legislation forbidding its existence.

And people who voluntarily help vacuums move along the floor should be publicly flogged. *All* people.

APRIL 30, 2004

The People are out ~~whoring around~~ shopping, and I'm here at home, all alone. My dish is nearly empty, I know it's got to be *hours* past my dinner time, and I'm starving. In fact, I think I've lost about half my body weight in the last 2 hours (ok, part of that was a giant poop I left in the litter box, but still…)

My Stinky Goodness is inside this plastic container on the counter (well, to be honest, it's on the floor under the table now) and I can't get it open, and believe me, I've tried.

There are treats in the drawer by the sink, and I know I can chew through the bag, but I can't get the drawer open either. Every time I get it just a tiny bit open, it snaps back.

I'd even go for the People food, but for once they actually put everything away.

I am going to die.
I just know it.

MAY 1, 2004

No matter what the People say, I did not run away when the bird outside flew right by the window.

I had to pee, and I had to pee *right then*.

I was *not* scared.
That was a damned big bird, though…

MAY 2, 2004

People…don't meow at your kitties.
You sound stupid, and you don't know what you're saying.
Plus, you have the accent all wrong.

MAY 3, 2004

Evidently, I was twitching a lot in my sleep this afternoon, enough that the Woman must have thought I was having some kind of seizure, because she woke me up. Holy guacamole, if I woke her up every time she moved in her sleep, I'd be busy all night long and neither one of us would get any sleep.

In her sterling intelligence, once my eyes were open she asked, "Were you dreaming?"

HELL YES WOMAN I WAS DREAMING!
Just what do you *expect* from a sleeping kitty?

I swear, tonight when her nose twitches, I am *so* going to pounce on her head, and when she sits up, I'll ask oh-so-sweetly, "Why, were you dreaming?"

Yeah, she'll probably think I'm asking for cuddles and she'll pick me up and start squeezing and getting all goofy.

I'd better eat really fast tonight, so that I have lots of potent gas.

MAY 4, 2004

I need to come up with new ways to get the Woman out of bed in the morning. The tried and true methods of peeling her lazy ass up just aren't working well anymore. This morning I tried them all—except for launching her glasses across the room, because I wanted to live through breakfast—and she just wouldn't open her freaking eyes. I know she knew I was there, because at one point she mumbled "Go away," but all she did was roll over and bury her face in the pillow. I even tried plopping down on top of her head, thinking that if she couldn't breathe, she'd *have* to get up, but no…she must have held her breath for a good 15 minutes. Her face was jammed down into that pillow and I was holding it there, but she never budged.

I shouldn't have to work so hard for my food. I need something that will get her out of bed at my first request. Yep, something reallllly good…

MAY 5, 2004

It's raining. That sucks. There's nothing good going on outside the window when it rains. No Sticky People to amuse me. No other cats. Even the People don't sit outside in their cheap plastic chairs and talk to each other. I need something to do in between naps, and the rain robs me of one of the few things in life I can do and not get in trouble over.

MAY 6, 2004

Holy Crap!
FRESH STINKY GOODNESS!!!

This didn't come from a can, but a real live dead fish that the Man brought home and cooked up just for me. He even threw it on the grill until it was nice and flaky, taste tested it to make sure it was good enough, and then gave me a *bowl full.*

If this is what happens when they disappear on me all day, they can leave more often. I'm so full my tummy hurts, but I can take the Woman's chair and sleep it off. I'm sure she'll be happy to sit somewhere else while I digest.

MAY 7, 2004

A leash?
No.
Just…no.
I am not a dog, I do not go for walks.
Don't. Even. Think. About. It.
I don't care if it belonged to the Cat Who Came Before Me.
Throw. It. Away.

MAY 8, 2004

It's all in the timing, folks.

The Woman came home from her afternoon of ~~heavy drinking~~ running errands, and just as she came through the door she heard me emit a funky kind of squeak.

So she goes tearing through the house, saying "Where are you, Max? Are you okay? Where are you?!"

Cripes, lady.

She finally found me, in the litter box.
Yeah, I was popping out a good one, and made a little noise.

You *know* it's a good one when your person screws up her face, covers her nose and says "Oh my God, what crawled up inside of you and died?"

Maybe that'll teach her to panic needlessly and invade my privacy.

MAY 9, 2004

Well…did *you* kick all that litter out of the box?
Who do you *think* did it?

Trust me, when you're not looking, I will be rolling my eyes like a frustrated teenager.

May 10, 2004

Okay Boys and Girls, here's another way to amuse yourself with your Humans.

They like to watch TV, and they all have those thingies they use to make the picture change, right? And a lot of the time they leave those thingies on the sofa.

So all you have to do is sit on the thingy—make sure it's pointed at the TV—and watch them get all upset trying to figure out what might be wrong with their precious idiot boxes.

It'll take them a good 2 minutes to realize you're the one sitting on the remote. You won't even get in trouble, and those 2 minutes are great fun.

May 11, 2004

On a different note… People, you have opposable thumbs. You can open any can in the house and feed yourselves. You can operate the hot box in the kitchen and cook up some perfectly wonderful, tasty treats. You can even pour odd smelling things out of a box and eat them. You don't need to wait for *someone* to drag their sorry ass out of bed to open a can of Stinky Goodness, as you can do it yourself.

So why, tell me why, would you sit there in a chair, starting at the idiot box in the living room, hungry? Why would you not just get up and get food? More importantly, why would you disturb *my* nap because of it?

Really, I'm curled up on the Woman while she sites there and watches some bald guy yell at people on TV, sound asleep, when this horrendous noise jolts me awake. I'm thinking "Holy crap, it's an earthquake!" but she's not concerned at all; she's just watching that damned TV. So I put my head down, and it happens again. It's her freaking stomach, and it's growling louder than a dog in the middle of a squirrel attack.

Did she get up to get food? Nooooo… that would be too easy. No, she just sat there like whatever the bald guy was saying was really important (it wasn't, trust me), and allowed my nap to be ruined by her unwillingness to put something in her stomach to quiet the noise.

Come on, people. I can't open my own cans, but *you* sure as hell can. And while you're at it, share. That stuff might not really be cat food, but it came out of a can and smells like cat food, so it must be cat-edible. Really now.

MAY 12, 2004

If you don't want me to play with your puzzle pieces, don't leave them on the table.

They don't taste very good, anyway.

MAY 13, 2004

Oh.
If you're in the mood to head butt something, your Human Male's crotch gets the best reaction.

Trust me on this.

MAY 14, 2004

I'm not sure I like this warmer weather. It's not like *I* get to go outside and enjoy it, and it keeps my People away from me. And it's not as if I really want them in here bugging me all the time, but they *should* be available to meet my needs as they arise.

The last few days have been especially trying—the Woman goes outside to "read" but then other People start showing up, and they sit in these cheap plastic chairs in a circle, talking and laughing and wrangling the Sticky Little Creatures. And for whatever reason, they seem to find the Sticky Ones appealing and somewhat humorous. Okay, I suppose it's cute to see the smallest of them trying to work up the nerve to take that first step. And the slightly older Sticky People sliding on that wet piece of plastic was kind of funny in a warped sort of way, especially after it was placed on the little hill and they had leverage to work up some speed.

But it still means *my* Woman is out *there* and not inside where she should be. And she freaking spends all day out there! What the heck can People talk about for so long, and for so many days??? Why aren't they inside taking care of the cats???

May 15, 2004

More good kitty fun…pick any closed door in the house, and sit in front of it and holler. Then start banging on it. When one of your People finally gets fed up, they'll open the door…but don't go through it. Turn around and walk away.

When they sit down and get comfortable, repeat the process with another door.

Do this as many times as you think you can get away with before really pissing them off.

May 16, 2004

Still more kitty fun.

Pick a point on the ceiling and stare up at it like there's something there. Your People will get up and look at the ceiling, too, trying to figure out what you see. They always think it's a bug or something gross, so they're always interested. You can keep them there for a good minute or so, staring at nothing.

May 17, 2004

I sat in the window today and watched the Woman outside. She was out there all freaking day long, digging in the dirt. If it had been me, I'd have gotten yelled at (I did get yelled at for running behind the big thing they have the TV on…hey People, if you don't want me back there, shove it against the wall!) but she just knelt there and dug. And planted a chitload of flowers. Like she knew what she was doing.

Now, they look okay, but does she not realize those things will just get bigger, and she'll have to remember to water them? They're doomed.

Not to mention, the outside cats around here will probably poop between the plants.

I would, but there's no way I'm going outside. There are Sticky People out there—even a *new* Sticky Little Person.

They're taking over the world.

May 18, 2004

Yeah, those pants make your ass look big.

Though I don't really think it has so much to do with the pants as it does the ass...

> Now I lay me down to sleep
> I pray that you will earn your keep
> By feeding me the things that Stink
> And fresh live dead stuff, good, I think.
> By keeping me in a killer haze
> With kitty crack, for all my days.
> If you can do this you will be
> Finally worthy of me.
>
> More good poetry by Max.

It hasn't been the best week yet.

Nothing inside the Woman's nose smells really bad.

I haven't been able to stick my nose in her ear.

Gas supplies are limited, so I'm not offensive enough.

No hairballs to puke up.

Nothing disgusting to deposit in the litter box while the Woman is in the bathroom...

No wonder I'm bored.

May 19, 2004

Not that I'm getting soft or anything, but I let the Woman sleep in a little bit today. I started to get her up at the appointed time by singing at the top of my little lungs, but when she didn't stir, I figured it was best to leave her alone. I mean, she was a source of amusement all night long, what with her odd snorting and gurgling sounds coming out of her nose. I wound up sitting on the bed just listening to her part of the night—how do people make those disgusting noises without waking themselves up?

And the smell! Holy crap, there's this stench coming out of her nose like you wouldn't believe...I kind of like it and am kind of repelled at the same time. It was stench-worthy of risking waking her up by cramming my nose up one of her nostrils for a minute, but I don't think that disturbed her. One eye opened and she did shove me off of her, but she didn't yell or anything. She just rolled over and started making new noises.

She finally got up about 45 minutes late this morning, and don't tell her I said this, but damn, she looked like hell. She must not remember my nose up hers, because she didn't yell or snap at me. In fact, she's just whispering for the most part.

This might be worth getting fed late.

MAY 20, 2004

I chased a bug across the floor today, and the way the People acted you'd have thought it was the menu for the next two weeks.

"Catch it, Max!"
"Get it!"
"Come on, you can do it!"

Yeah.

I *know* I can catch the stupid bug. I never said I *wanted* to catch it. Sometimes the thrill is in the chase, you know? I scare the crap out if it, let it get somewhere it thinks it's safe, and can come back and terrorize it again later. Maybe even rip off a leg or two.

But sheesh…the way they acted it was like if I didn't catch it, I wasn't going to get to eat today.

I *am* going to get to eat today.
Aren't I?

MAY 21, 2004

The Woman doesn't understand why, after the Man has fed me in the morning, I still feel the need to come into the bedroom, sit by the door, and make a lot of noise.

Well, I don't understand why after she'd been asleep all freaking night, she still feels the need to stay in bed, being completely nonproductive.

And it's not *noise* that I'm making. I'm singing. And she doesn't seem to appreciate it, not one bit. And really "Get Your Fat Ass Out Of Bed You Lazy Human" is a very fine song.

She doesn't appreciate "Make The Damned Bed Already So I Can Take A Sweet, Sweet Nap," either.

The solution is simple: get up! You get up, and I'll shut up, and we'll both be happy!

MAY 22, 2004

If you have to ask if you're disturbing my nap, you probably are.

MAY 23, 2004

Here's a lesson learned: if you're on your Human's lap, and you hear the sound of thunder rolling from their tummy, get up and run before they stand up and dump you onto the floor.

A tummy sounding like that can only mean one thing: you do *not* want to go into the bathroom for a long, long time.

Trust me.

MAY 24, 2004

I have a bump on my nose.

It's probably just a bug bite or a tiny zit, but the way the People are acting you'd think I have nose cancer and my face is about to fall off.

I hope the next time one of them gets a zit and I'm all over their face, trying to pop the damn thing, they'll remember this day.

You do not mess with my face.
Not unless you want little kitty presents in your shoes and on your pillows.

MAY 25, 2004

The People get to choose what they have for dinner every night.

Do they ever ask me what I want? Really, they just open a can and plop it onto my plate (one of their plates I might add...I don't even get my own freaking plate) and assume it's what I'm in the mood for.

You know, some nights I might want chicken Stinky Goodness.
Other nights I might want fishy Stinky Goodness.

Most nights I want what they're having, but no. It seems like everything they eat is either bad for kitties or makes flames shoot out your ass. I've *never* seen flames shoot out their asses (though sometimes they have to light a candle in the bathroom...) And it can't be too bad because neither one of them has dropped dead yet.

They could at least share.
And give me shrimp every night.

MAY 26, 2004

There's not a whole lot to do at night for a cat when a cat can't sleep. So don't ask me *why* I decided 3 a.m. was a good time to play with your feet. It's not like I had anything better to do.

MAY 27, 2004

I am not on your lap to show how much I love you.
I am not nuzzling your face out of affection.
I am not wiggling on my back to be cute.

I am on your lap because it's there.
I am nuzzling your face because that gets hair up your nose.
I am wiggling on my back because you are wearing brand new black jeans, and the wiggling transfers a ton of fur onto them in just seconds.

All of this annoys you, and that amuses me.

MAY 28, 2004

They smell like dog.
The people came home and they *smell like dogs*.
Unacceptable.

May 29, 2004

Okay.

How come the People can occasionally eat cat food, but they give me fits over me eating People food? I *know* the Man had cat food tonight. He opened a can, and on the outside it said T-U-N-A, and that spells cat food. Maybe not in the literal sense, but I've seen it on my little cans of Stinky Goodness a hundred times. So I *know* it's cat food. And it's the good stuff. Plus it was a *huge* can.

He gave me some of the liquid out of the cat, but only a small bite of the tuna. So he gets to eat a whole can of Premium Stinky Goodness, but do I ever get to sit down with an entire roast beef or plate full of tacos?

Yeah, yeah, yeah, flames out the ass and all that.

I hope he gets third degree burns on his.
Or at least an itchy case of hemorrhoids.

May 30, 2004

I have issues this weekend.
The Woman keeps leaving the house and returns still smelling of dog.
I can hear her outside calling to them.
If she brings one home, that's it.
The pooping on the pillows shall commence.

May 31, 2004

Ok, I don't know what the hell this is:

but there are half a dozen of them outside my window, and I don't like it, not one bit. They don't speak, don't blink; they just stand there and stare. Worse, I don't even think they're edible.

What good is an inedible bird???

JUNE 1, 2004

Why is everything that smells good "not for kitties?" If it's not good for kitties, what the hell makes you think it's good for People? Like that red stuff you People have been drinking…obviously, it's not good for you.

I've been watching. The People have been sitting outside with the other people, their ample butts plastered in the plastic chairs, they have lights on in the tree, and they keep coming in the house to make these red drinks in the blender.

And you know what? As the night goes on, they just get louder and stupider. They start laughing, they send the Sticky Little People away, and they Just.Get.Stupid.

Do they not see the correlation?
Red drinks + People = Stupidity
Obviously, they've had a lot of red drinkage over time…

JUNE 2, 2004

Here's the good thing about having fur: no clothes. And since I don't wear clothes, I never have to suffer the indignation of standing in the bathroom with a cat watching, as I try to figure out how I put my shirt on backwards, and then muck it up when trying to rearrange it.

JUNE 3, 2004

I am not fat.
I am voluptuous.
Yes, fourteen pounds of voluptuous black and white fur.
I'm beautiful, and you better acknowledge it, baby.

JUNE 4, 2004

Doesn't it make sense that if a person is going to reach down from their chair to pet a kitty, that they would look to see where their hand is?

Yeah, I saw the hand headed right for my face—that was an eye-poked-out waiting to happen—so I turned and the Woman grabbed a handful of sleek black cat butt.

How is that my fault...?

JUNE 5, 2004

I haven't had the chance to catch one of those incredibly ugly birds that have made the front yard their home, but I still intend to. I keep looking out at them, and they're all pretty big, which theoretically means a hell of a lot of meat on their bones. It's possible they're not inedible after all. I want to find out.

And the People wised up; they no longer return smelling of dog, though the Woman came in yesterday (after being out there in a chair on the front lawn *all freaking day*, leaving me here all alone) smelling kind of funky. I think it was the smell of Sticky Little People. If she brings one of *those* home, not only will I poop on her pillow, but I might have to hack up a hairball or two, carefully placed deep enough in her shoes where she won't see it right off the bat.

JUNE 6, 2004

If I'm standing next to my dry food dish, and I am raising a fuss, *and* the person can see the bottom of said dish, doesn't it stand to reason that the person would put food in that dish?

Hell no, *that* would make sense...

JUNE 7, 2004

They're both drinking tonight.
And that's not a lie.
Red drinks, both of them.

They better not "forget" to feed me.

JUNE 8, 2004

Shrimpy Goodness!!!
Yes!

June 9, 2004

Look…if I think that what you're having for dinner smells intriguing, chances are I'm going to jump up onto the table and see for myself. Getting your shorts in a wad is not going to change that. Pointing your finger at me and making threats doesn't faze me. You might as well get over it already. It's going to happen again, I assure you.

June 10, 2004

So, back to the dog we used to have. I thought about him today, because when I was laying on my window perch, soaking up some sun, I saw another dog that looked a lot like him. I mean, so much so that I had to sit up and *really* look. I had that brief thought that maybe the People gave him away, but then I remembered that they treated him like he was a Person—even cooking *real food* for him, something they *never* do for me—and that they wouldn't give him to anyone else.

But thinking about him and all the fuss they made over him, especially those last few weeks before he disappeared, it makes me wonder—why do people like dogs so much anyway? They poop on the grass, so that has to be picked up (a litter box is so much more convenient, it seems.) They have to be walked, apparently because they're not quite bright enough to find their way back home on their own. They let people tell them when to sit, stand, lay down roll over…

Well. That's probably it. They feed the Human need to think they're in charge. At least with cats they know better.

Still, I saw that other dog today and I think I kind of missed him. I'm not sure why—I went to great lengths to avoid him most of the time—but I watched that other dog and wondered why I can't have him back. And the Woman noticed me watching and said she misses him, too.

No, this time I didn't get all fuzzy and warm and cuddle her sad self. This time I got down, stretched, farted in her general direction, and went to get some dry food.

She wasn't *that* sad.
And I have a reputation to maintain.

JUNE 11, 2004

If you knock a thingy off the bathroom counter, and it's the thingy that has something the Woman sticks into her arm every night, and you break it, well, she gets mighty upset.

And if you're in the bathroom, chances are the door is closed and there's nowhere to run.

It's a good thing she's not prone to beatings…

But really, she knew I was on the counter, and that thingy was all shiny under the light, and she knows I'm attracted to bright shiny things, so it stands to reason that I was going to try to play with it.

How was I supposed to know it was glass? Or that it's "very, very expensive medication?" (That's People for "Them's *my* drugs, cat!") It's not my fault that she put it where I could get to it.

Playing with shiny things, that's my job.
She should know that.

JUNE 12, 2004

I keep looking into the dry food dish, not because I'm always that hungry.

I look because I have high hopes that someday it will be filled with Shrimpy Goodness and not dry, brittle crap.

It's the same reason People keep looking into the pantry; they *know* what's in there, but they keep hoping a box of Ding Dongs will magically appear.

JUNE 13, 2004

The People can't figure out how they can do laundry, fold the clothes and put them away, and yet still have cat hair all over everything.

The People haven't figured out that if there's a drawer open, I am going to crawl in it and curl up on every thing I possible can.

The People aren't especially intelligent, are they?

JUNE 14, 2004

I don't know the fuss is all about. The toilet paper is still there, still available for the People to use.

So it's unrolled.
So what?

JUNE 15, 2004

No, getting up on the counter and knocking everything to the floor is not a game.
It's a birthright.

JUNE 16, 2004

The Woman could not sleep last night, and it wasn't even my fault. I didn't wake her up by singing to her, and I didn't plop myself down over her face. She just couldn't sleep.

So, she got up and turned on the computer and started playing online...not once did she stop to think that she was keeping *me* up. Yeah, sure, I could have stayed in bed, but she went into the kitchen first so I had to go see, just in case there was food to be given out. After I was sure I wasn't getting anything, I did go back to bed.

And dammit, there she was an hour later, climbing back into bed, waking me up. And she turned the freaking TV on, which just made it worse.

I got even, though. When she was trying to sleep in this morning, I sang my little heart out. Plus I had to fart a lot, so I made sure I did that close enough to her head that she couldn't ignore it. There was a lot of swearing, and threats of throwing things at me, but I've learned those are empty threats. To throw something she'd have to get her ass out of bed, and that would take too much effort.

Once she got up, I curled up right smack dab in the middle of the bed and took a nap. Just because I could.

June 17, 2004

Do *not* keep calling me "Sir Poopsalot."
You crap more than I do. The only difference is you can flush.

June 18, 2004

No, I was not head butting the bathroom door in order to get in.
The top of my head itched.
That's all.

June 19, 2004

You know, it's really not necessary to ask a cat why he's doing whatever he's doing. Just ignore it, go along with it, or gush about how cute it is. But don't ask why, because you'll never understand. It's a cat thing.

I had this really long black twist tie I was playing with today—it was a shit load of fun, getting to pounce on it and throw it and chase it. But the Woman just got this puzzled look and asked me why I like to play with twist ties.

Well hell, why *wouldn't* I like to play with them?

I told her I was just playing with it until she wasn't looking, then I was going to get all stabby on her with the sharp end, but she ignored that. Like she didn't even understand.

June 20, 2004

Hey. If I don't like being called Sir Poopsalot, you can be pretty sure I don't like being called "Drama Queen," either.

I was starving and I just wanted to let you know about it.
So sue me.

June 21, 2004

They did not feed me this morning!

I'm not kidding—they left the house without giving me my half a can of Stinky Goodness. The Woman says she thought the Man had fed me, and evidently he thought she had… Don't these People know how to coordinate? Are they *stupid???*

I damn near starved today!

Even after they came home and I started hollering at them, what did they do? They went outside and sat in those stupid chairs, waving at me through the window, saying stupid things like "Hi, Max," and "You're fine, Max."

I was *not* fine!
I was *dying!*

At 5 o'clock the Woman finally said she'd feed me, and was freaking *surprised* when there was no half a can left to give to me. Well Jesus Christ on a Pogo Stick, what was she expecting? I can't open the &^%^%$ cans by myself.

I thought I had them trained.
They are so unworthy of living with me.
Really.

June 22, 2004

She obviously feels bad.

This morning I got my can of Stinky Goodness early; she rolled out of bed at an acceptable hour, and didn't make me wait. She came right downstairs without using the Giant Litter box and fed me.

And later, before she and the Man went to sit outside, she gave me some crunchy treats.

Oh yeah, she feels bad.
And that's fine with me.

June 23, 2004

Lots of cats like to be brushed. I am not one of them. Not at all.

The People know this; they've tried off and on over the last couple of years to groom my already perfect coif, and it ends the same way every time. One of us is pissed off, and the other is bleeding.

So what does the Woman try yet again?

Cripes. There's a reason I try to chew that stupid little brush into pieces every time I see it. What's the thrill? Why try so hard to do something to me that doesn't need to be done? I've got short hair, Peoples, it doesn't tangle and I keep it pretty freaking clean, so lay off!

Just wait until she's snoozing and I try to groom *her* hair. See how she likes *that*.

JUNE 24, 2004

Um, do I want to go outside?
It's *raining*, and this is what she asks me.
Sarcastic witch widda B.

JUNE 25, 2004

Just as good as a twist tie: the ring off of a jug of milk. Those are loads of fun to play with, plus they smell like food for the first few hours. After that they kind of stink, like a Sticky Little Person who's just belched up breakfast, but those first few hours are awesome.

My people don't drink much milk, though, so I don't get to play with them very often. And when I do, I have to dig them out of the trash because no one seems to take half a minute to think that the cat might want it to bat around for a while.

Think of your cats, People. At least think of someone besides yourselves for once.

JUNE 26, 2004

Well, no, your book does not make a particularly comfortable pillow, but the sheer joy of annoying the crap out of you makes using it worthwhile.

JUNE 27, 2004

I did *not* try to cuddle with the Woman at 2:30 this morning.
I absolutely did not.

I only jumped up onto the bed and curled up on her chest to shove fur up her nose. The fact that it involved having to rub my face against hers repeatedly is only coincidental. I was just trying to annoy her with massive amounts of fur.

That is all.

JUNE 28, 2004

When the Sticky Little People play outside my window, and they want something, the Old People tell them to say "please" and then they get whatever it is they're whining about (except for the really small ones, who point and grunt and get it.)

So I tried this. I sat in the kitchen and said "please" over and over and over—for about an hour—but did it do me any good?

All I got was "No, Max." "It's too early, Max." "You're not going to starve to death, Max."

What good is PLEASE if it doesn't work?

I could stand there and say "Feed me now or I'll gouge your eyes out" and get the same results.

I'm cuter than the Sticky Little People. I must be doing something wrong.

JUNE 29, 2004

If you clip a kitties claws, they are no longer sharp.
If they are no longer sharp, a kitty must sharpen them.
To sharpen them, a kitty must scratch at something, preferably something you love.
So if you don't want a kitty to scratch, stop clipping our freaking claws!

JUNE 30, 2004

It feels like it's way past my dinner time—I know because my tummy is growling like crazy and I'm =this= close to passing out right here in the computer chair—but the Woman keeps saying "No, it's not time yet. You have to wait."

So what does she do? The bitch pops a piece of chocolate into her mouth!

I have to wait, but apparently the Queen of All Things MEAN doesn't.

I wish I had a hairball to hack up, because I'd aim right for her bright white shoes.

JULY 1, 2004

Oh man.
There are bugs out here with LIGHTBULBS in their asses.
Seriously!
I saw them last night while I was looking out the window.
I think they need new ones, or at least new batteries, though, because they just keep flashing on and off.

JULY 2, 2004

Yes, that's a dead cricket on the floor.
Yes, I ripped its legs off.
What about it?

JULY 3, 2004

Ugh.
Lesson learned: water in the bathtub after the Man takes a bath is *not* drinkable.
Nasty…just nasty.

JULY 4, 2004

Let's talk about bugs. All the flies and spiders that seem to have found their way into the house.

Look, just because I'm a cat, that doesn't mean I'm going to eat them. I get enough Stinky Goodness and that dry crap left out for snacking between meals. I don't need the extra protein I could get from slurping down the dead carcass of a eight legged freak or the wiggling body of a no-longer flying trash monger.

Now, sure, I take great joy in hunting them down, and ripping off their little wings and legs, but I'm not going to eat them.

I've effectively removed them from being an irritant.

Isn't that enough?

JULY 5, 2004

Hey, not only does my entire nose fit into just one of the Woman's nostrils, it also fits neatly into one of her ears. But if you try this with your Human, be warned: if you inhale hard enough, you get icky things in your nose.

JULY 6, 2004

Oh!

I was looking outside and I saw a ball on the ground, and it wasn't just *any* ball. It was silvery and shiny, and I wanted to play with it. I got the Woman's attention, and she came to the window to look, and she even knew exactly what I was getting excited about, but did she go outside and get that shiny ball for me?

Hell no.

She just laughed and said it wasn't mine, but surely I really had lost a few marbles along the way.

Just get me the shiny ball already!

JULY 7, 2004

I'm not sure what the People had for lunch (since they weren't home when they had it…big surprise there…) but judging from their breaths, it was awfully good. Just the smell has made me hungry, but will they get off their behinds and feed me?

"It's not time."

God, I hate that. Those three words are like fingernails on a chalkboard.

Feed me already!
Feed me before I get postal on your asses!

July 8, 2004

How to get the Woman to gag:

Barf up a copious furball immediately after dinner. She'll choke and gag as she tries to clean it up, eventually giving up the effort to the Man.

And best yet, she says I'll get more dinner later, because my tummy must be empty now.
Score!

July 9, 2004

If there's something good in the trash can, you can be sure it will get knocked over.
That's physics.
Cat physics.

(Good Food + Awesome Stink)Trash Can = Mess To Clean Up^2
Or maybe it's Cat Math.

Whatever…leave me something good in the trash can, and I'm going to get to it, one way or another.

July 10, 2004

Rice Krispy treats are kind of tasty.

I'm not supposed to know this—it's not like I was offered any, even though I made it clear that they smelled pretty good—but when the Woman left them to cool on the counter I jumped up and licked them all.

Hey, first come, first serve.
And it's not like I have cooties, she *could* have still eaten them.

As she was throwing them away she muttering something about me licking my own ass, but, whatever.

July 11, 2004

I've been nice the last couple of mornings; I've let the Woman sleep in almost as late as she wants. Yesterday she rolled over and looked at the clock, and pretty much sat straight up, apologizing to me for sleeping in and being so late with my breakfast.

This morning she slept even later, and didn't wake up until I curled up on top of her and pawed at her nose. Hey, I was nice, it was a gentle nudge to let her know that any later and it would be time for dinner. Or a snack, at the very least.

She's very grateful when I let her sleep late. While the "oh you're such a good boy" crap makes me want to puke, if I ignore it I can be pretty sure I'll get a bite or two of whatever they have for their dinner. Even if I jump up on the table to check it out while they're eating.

Tonight they had ham, and even though I leaped up to get a good look, I got a bite. Not as much as I wanted, or even as much as I think she would have given me, but she said "I'm not sure how much pork kitties can have."

Hey, it's dead and it's meat—preferably cooked—I can eat it.

I haven't decided how late I'll let her sleep tomorrow. Depends on if I can figure out what the menu for tomorrow night is.

~ ~ ~

Potato soup is quite tasty, especially when the person you got it from doesn't know you tasted it.

July 12, 2004

I did my feline-ly duty last night.

The Woman was lying in bed last night, watching that idiot box, when I spotted something crawling on top of her. So I pounced—garnering a loud "Oof!" from her—and saved her from the terribly hairy and giant spider that was making its way up towards her face.

I grabbed it, jumped off the bed, and ripped off its ugly little legs.

She owes me now, in a big way.
That was just nasty tasting.
Seriously, seriously gross.

JULY 13, 2004

All right. I think we've been over this before but it obviously bears repeating because the People don't seem to get it.

If you leave your shirt, or pants, or anything else on the bed, it becomes part of the bed, and therefore I am entitled to take a nap on it.

If you have a problem with that, MOVE YOUR FREAKING CLOTHES!

JULY 14, 2004

Why is your magazine in my litter box?
Well...*you* read when you're using your litter box, why shouldn't I?
If it bothers you, fish it out.

JULY 15, 2004

How complicated does life have to be? You get up—use the giant litter box if you must, though I'd prefer you waited—open my can of Stinky Goodness, then get dressed and make the bed so that I have a place to nap.

When you get up, get dressed, make the bed, use the litter box, and make me wait for breakfast, my whole routine is destroyed and I'm off kilter the rest of the day.

Your clothes can wait!
The bed can wait!
Pee yourself for all I care, but FEED ME FIRST!

Isn't that simple?
Do you need to write it down?

JULY 16, 2004

If there's a basket on the floor, and I climb in, do *not* laugh and say I'm a basket case.
Your favorite shoes just might meet a toothy death.

JULY 17, 2004

Looking in the closet, there's a basket full of shoes. Even a pair of Nike's.
Well, now.
I believe I'll Just Do It.
Right in those shoes…

JULY 18, 2004

The People had clothes in the dryer, and I was waiting happily for the clothes
to come out, but they just left them there. All night long. A whole bunch of
clothes in the dryer, where I can't roll around in them.

What's the point of drying clothes and then leaving them so the kitty can't
have something warm to play in?

Selfish, selfish people…

JULY 19, 2004

Awesomeness!
Sweet!
Check it out!

A box you can see through!

My People brought this home last week, and in spite of what you might think—
like what's the point of a box you can't hide in—this one is loads of fun.

Think about it: you can't hide in it, but that also means you can see People sneaking up on you. Never again will I have to suffer through People who think they're oh-so-clever tip toe'ing up to the box I'm resting in, pounding on the top and laughing like they've just done something funny (hey, People, it's *mean*. How would you like it if Giganticor started thumping on the top of your bedroom while you're trying to sleep? You'd pee yourself and start screaming like little girls.) I can lounge in my box and *see* anyone trying to approach!

You gotta wonder…why didn't they invent this sooner???

JULY 20, 2004

Oh. Don't try to jump on your people right after they've gotten the mail, especially if it's from someone named "Bill."

Whatever Bill has to say, they don't like it, and they have *no* sense of humor then.

JULY 21, 2004

For once I think I would like to sit in the Woman's lap, but no, she's "busy."

Well, busy to me looks a lot like just sitting on her fat behind, tapping away at the computer, with the TV playing in the background. And that bald guy is talking again. I swear, what he has to say is not nearly as important as providing a lap and some head scratching for a kitty.

She better change her mind soon, because I don't get in the mood for this very often. Just watch, later on she'll be all "oh let's love on da kitty" and I'm going to want to scratch her eyes out.

Only they had me declawed when they had my nads cut off, so I can't even do *that*!

JULY 22, 2004

Yeah, I jumped.

Yeah, it was straight up off the ottoman, and I'm pretty sure my heart skipped 2 or 3 beats while my fur stood up on end, but it was *loud*. I mean, so loud that

I expected to look outside the front window and see the house across the street up in flames. It sounded like *something* blew up, and I'm not a wussy kitty for reacting to it.

But no, the Man has to laugh.
Well screw you!
How was I supposed to know it was lightning?
I don't even know what that *is*!

July 23, 2004

Yo...

July 24, 2004

Eww.

The People came home a little while ago, and I jumped up into the Woman's lap to sniff and see what she'd had for lunch. Holy crap, I think she sucked on an onion for an hour. My eyes started to water, and if I hadn't jumped down I'm pretty sure my nose would have started to bleed.

I'm staying away from her the rest of the day, because if what they keep telling me is true, sooner or later she's gonna have flames shooting out her ass, and I'm pretty sure my fur is flammable.

Contrary to what the People say, I am not a motor mouth.
I just have to talk a lot to get them to feed me.

Every day, I swear it takes about an hour to get them up and into the kitchen. If they'd get up at the first request, then I wouldn't have to talk so much.

If I'm not hungry, I'm pretty quiet.

But yeah, I'm hungry a lot.
They need to feed me more.

JULY 25, 2004

Yeah, okay.
You gave me fresh catnip, and *alot* of it, so what did you expect?
That I'd curl up and be a good kitty?
Face it, a bag of kitty crack and a very full dish of dry food pretty much means you're going to have a big mess to clean up.
Don't expect my help; I'm busy sleeping it off.

JULY 26, 2004

Flames
Will
Not
Shoot
Out
My
Ass
So give it to me already!!!

JULY 27, 2004

I read this thing on someone else's blog today; it talked about how someone else had complained that blogs were becoming nothing but places where people post pictures of and talk about their cats.

So?

Is that a problem?

You don't see me bitching about how most blogs are boring diatribes on the political process, something those writing about it seem to really know very little.

If you don't like reading cat stuff, then don't.
And you can kiss my shiny black and white ass on your way out.

JULY 28, 2004

You'd think a person would be impressed with a cat's sense of balance, but evidently, if you're balanced on top of their chest while they're trying to sleep, they're not impressed at all. In fact, they get a little snarky about it.

JULY 29, 2004

The Woman got a paper cut on her thumb.

Ordinarily, I wouldn't give a rat's ass, but what if this means she can't open a can of Stinky Goodness in the morning? And what if the Man isn't home to do it? I might starve!

JULY 30, 2004

She's doing it again.

She's coming home smelling like *dog*. And I'm pretty sure I know which dog now, too. The other day I was looking out the back window, just minding my own freaking business, and this yappy little thing came out of nowhere and started growling at me.

Yeah, big brave doggy.

If she brings him home, there will be a revolt.
And the revolt will involve things coming out of my body.
From both ends.
I swear.

JULY 31, 2004

We are out of crunchy treats.

I know this because the Woman went into the kitchen and was going to give me some, but she opened the drawer where they usually are, and just said, "Sorry, we're all out."

Sorry?
Sorry?

Go out and get me some more!

Sheesh.

AUGUST 1, 2004

They ask me the dumbest questions sometimes. Like tonight; I was sitting on the Woman's lap while she watched some TV, and I felt the sudden need to bite something. Well, her arm wasn't too far off, so I lunged and tried to chomp down. Just a little bit. Not enough to draw blood.

Well, the way she acted you'd think I tried to gnaw one of her nipples off! She picked me up and dumped me onto the floor and then asked, "Why did you just do that?"

Duh.
Because I can.
Why do I do anything?

AUGUST 2, 2004

Isn't one cat enough?
I heard the people talking about getting another cat.
Why? Did I do something wrong?

I hope they don't mean to REPLACE me.
They wouldn't last a week without me here.
They'd be in bed all freaking day. Probably die there.

AUGUST 3, 2004

Um. Yeah. It was me who ripped open the pouch of catnip. Oh, look! A butterfly! I would really like a treat right now, or a whole handful of treats. Oh, look! Wait. Um. Yeah, it was me.

AUGUST 4, 2004

When cornered by a human who demands to know what you were just doing because they heard a noise that shouldn't have been, sit back, lift a leg, and start licking yourself. They have nothing to say to that.

AUGUST 5, 2004

Look, don't ask me why I scratch at things when I don't have any front claws. I just do. Not everything in life has to have a reason, you know. Like those clothes you're wearing. There can't be a good reason for those. Unless you got into my kitty crack before you went shopping. That would explain things, but still...

AUGUST 6, 2004

I swear, the Woman ate a can of my Stinky Goodness for her dinner tonight. Oh, she kept telling me to back off, that it wasn't cat food, but I'm not stupid. It came out of a can like my food, it looked like my food, and smelled like my food. Do the math! *She ate my food!* Even worse, I think she ate a can of the good stuff, and gave me some of the mediocre stuff for my dinner. Pretty freaking selfish, if you ask me.

AUGUST 7, 2004

Oh.
I think there really might be flames shooting out my ass.
When the People say "Picante sauce is not for kitties," I think they really mean it.

I think I shall go sit on the Woman's lap, and share...

AUGUST 8, 2004

Why did I knock the egg off the counter and onto the floor?
Because I could.

AUGUST 9, 2004

I can see in the dark, you know. Waiting until you turn out the light to pick your nose doesn't change that.

AUGUST 10, 2004

Don't keep the kitty up all night. Just because you can't sleep doesn't mean I shouldn't sleep. Stay in bed and pretend. Just be quiet. I don't need beauty sleep—I just need sleep—but you at *least* need beauty rest.

Okay, I know the People have this weird thing about getting into a tub full of water, or standing there under a spray of water. They're too lazy to lick themselves clean, so they do this instead.

But, cripes. People. Leave your clothes on. I sat there in the bathroom today and watched the Woman peel off her clothes, and all I could think was "Ewww," and "Grow some hair, Lady!" Naked people look like cats who got caught in a nuclear blast. You're all mutants, you know that, don't you?

Adding to the complete bizarreness of it all—what little fur the Woman DOES manage to grow, she shaves off! Well, most of it. What the hell? The one thing you People have that might help you look a little less odd, and it gets shaved off.

Just do us all a favor and keep the clothes on. I'm sure they need to be washed, too, and you'd be taking care of two things at once by bathing in them.

AUGUST 12, 2004

Well son of a—!

The Woman was surfing around online and came across an tidbit she just *had* to share with me. And now I am completely bummed out.

Evidently, there's something in Tuna that causes it to block Thiamin in kitties, and if given too much it can make them very, very sick. So kitties can have a bite of tuna here and there, but not on a regular basis. If you want to give your kitty tuna, it should be tuna cat food.

But people tuna is *so* much better!!! It has all the fishy goodness a kitty could want, plus it stinks so wonderfully!

She also informed me that a steady diet of dog food can make a cat go blind because it lacks taurine.

Whoopty do. Like I wanted dog food anyway.
I want tuna!

AUGUST 13, 2004

I just saw the mother of all flies. It had to be about the size of the tip of a Human's thumb. No kidding—it buzzed like bee, and I'm surprised it could even fly as big as it was. I chased it around the house a little bit, mostly because I just couldn't believe a fly could get that big, but there was no way I was going to take a bite out of that thing.

Flies that big have to have something wrong…one bite and I might have died. Or at least barfed, and not in a fun way.

AUGUST 14, 2004

Driving the Woman nuts is so freaking easy. All I have to do is follow her everywhere, and plop down right at her feet. If she goes into the bathroom, I race to get in there before she can close the door and I body slam myself at her feet. If she goes into the kitchen, there I am. To the room with my computer that I let her use…yep, you guessed it. Right smack dab on her feet.

She keeps asking me what my problem is, but hey, I'm just having fun. She seems to be the one with the problem.

I think next I'll start licking her.
That'll freak her out.

AUGUST 15, 2004

I look inside the refrigerator when you have it open because I can.
It doesn't matter if it's full of People Food or not.
It doesn't matter if the only thing in there is the bubbly water.
If the door is open, I will try to stick my head inside.
Because I can.

AUGUST 16, 2004

Once more…if it's on the counter, it's mine to do with as I wish, until you catch me or it's broken. That includes eggs, tomatoes, (well, anything rolly), ice cubes (even if they're still in the glass) or stray bits of cereal. Clean up more often, and you won't have a problem, right?

August 17, 2004

The difference between birds and bugs, even though they both fly:

I'd eat a bird if it got into the house.
Birds look like they'd be quite tasty, with lots of meat under those feathers.
Bugs…bleh. I'd rather lick my own ass.

August 18, 2004

I figured that if asking wasn't getting me anywhere, I'd try telepathy. So I climbed onto the Woman's lap, crawled up her chest, and set my forehead against hers, thinking, "treat…treat…treat."

Her skull is so thick I don't think she heard a thing. The only thing that happened—she screwed up her face and informed me that my breath is less than desirable.

She should talk.

August 19, 2004

So, I've been looking out the window a lot. The other day another one of those big ass trucks showed up, and with it came new people. *New Sticky Little People.* I think they're here to replace a couple other Sticky Little People who seem to have gone missing. I kind of liked one of the missing ones; she was very small but could say my name and didn't make any obnoxious shrieking sounds at me. She's one of the ones whom I allowed brief touching of my fur; she was very respectful and quiet and did not pull anything that should not be pulled.

But these new ones…I don't know about them. I haven't seen a whole lot and they so far have not played in front of my window, so we'll see.

The Woman says not to worry because we won't be here long enough for me to worry about them

Well hell.

I think I need to worry about THAT.

August 20, 2004

Hey. When a cat is cleaning himself, especially *cleaning* himself, you shouldn't make any loud startling noises. A kitty could do damage to himself, you know.

August 21, 2004

The Woman would not let me have a bite of chocolate pudding; she said if I had too much chocolate, I could go blind.

Well…I notice *she* can't see without those coke-bottle glasses.

Maybe cats aren't the only people who should avoid chocolate.

August 22, 2004

I did *not* say I was a people, I did *not* say I was a people…!

August 23, 2004

There's this thing on the ceiling, it's round and it has a red light in it. The red light doesn't do a whole lot of good, not even at night. I've been wondering what that thing is for, and tonight I found out.

It means dinner is done…and the People are going to eat out instead.

August 24, 2004

When the man in the brown trucks brings a box, the least he could do is make sure it's a big enough box for a cat to play in.

This thing…pitiful.

August 25, 2004

You know, it doesn't matter if it's 3 a.m. If you're up, and you're getting a snack, you should share! Cats get hungry in the middle of the night, too, and it would be nice to have something to nibble besides that dry crud left out to get all gnarly and stale.

Steak would be nice.
Even at 3 a.m.

AUGUST 26, 2004

Do I need a reason for stretching out across the hallway floor?

AUGUST 27, 2004

The reason I like the crinkly bag—especially in the middle of the night?

Duh.

Because.
It.
Crinkles.

AUGUST 28, 2004

Holy freaking crap. If the bug needs to be eaten, *you* eat it.
I'll rip the wings and legs off for you, but dammit, I am *not* eating it.
Be my guest.
Munch away.

AUGUST 29, 2004

Whatever a bowling ball is, I doubt I weigh that much. Yet when I jumped smack dab into the middle of the Woman's stomach today, that's what she said—that it was like getting slammed with a bowling ball. She also said she could prove it to me, because she has a bowling ball.

Well…I've been waiting all day, and I have not seen this bowling ball at all. So either she was lying and she doesn't want me to see it, or she exaggerated way out of proportion. She does that, you know. She says she weighs as much as the car, but I've been *in* the car, and honestly, I don't think the car weighs all that much.

There are bigger cars out there, but I haven't seen too many people bigger than my Humans.

But, back to the bowling ball.

If such a thing does exist, I figure it has to be in one of the closets, and I'd like to go exploring and see for myself, but they've developed the nasty habit of actually closing the doors. Well, the Man doesn't—he leaves the closet in his computer room open—but the Woman walks around closing doors and turning off lights. It's like that's her job now or something. Some kind of special training for the unemployable, I think. But it means I can't get into a closet to look.

I was in the great big bedroom closet yesterday, and I didn't see any balls. Just a ton of shoes (and they all smell like rubber) and some blankets, and more sweatshirts than a cat could possibly count. But no balls.

I looked into the Man's closet, but he doesn't have any balls, either.

The office closet was open a little bit…nothing there. There's really only one closet left where it would be, and I don't think that's ever open. If a bowling ball is gonna be anywhere, that has to be where.

Somehow, I've got to get that door open.

I think I'll go knock a toy under it when one of the People can see, and then I'll sit there and bitch about it until they open the door.

But I bet I'm not as big as it is.
Nope.

August 30, 2004

In all her infinite wisdom, today the Woman told me—regarding where I nap—to "Pick a place."

I did already.

I picked the big bed with the fuzzy cat blanket, the chair by the computer, the comfy chair, the sofa, the Man's favorite chair, the counter in the bathroom, the middle of the floor, the special seat at the window, and any sun spot I happen to encounter.

Sheesh, people. Pay attention.

AUGUST 31, 2004

The Woman is annoying me this week.

First, she breaks my computer. She *says* it was because of a power surge, but I know better. She broke it, and now I'm forced to try to type on this *laptop* computer. You know what? It sure as hell doesn't fit on *my* laptop.

Second, she won't stop coughing. What a royal pain in the butt. I'm trying to sleep on top of her chest, and she starts hacking away—it's like trying to sleep on a trampoline with a bunch of kids bouncing up and down on the other side. She damn near launched me across the room! And if I'm trying to snooze in the living room, here she comes, making those obnoxious wheezing and honking sounds, scaring me out of a deep sleep.

There's no consideration around here.

And they still keep talking about "the move." It sounds ominous, and I don't think I'm going to like it one bit.

SEPTEMBER 1, 2004

Getting a running start for an early morning wake-up head butt is very effective...it gets a Person out of bed in record time, let me tell you. They don't like it, but it's good for them. Really.

SEPTEMBER 2, 2004

I don't care if there's a fly buzzing around you, annoying you. I am not going to catch it for you, and I'm certainly not going to eat it for you. If it bothers you so much, roll up a newspaper and whack its little brains out, just don't expect me to get it simply because I'm a cat. I don't eat bugs. Haven't we gone over this before? If I'm in the mood, I might catch it and rip its wings off, but I will not eat it. I am not currently in the mood to de-wing a fly. Got that?

~ ~ ~

I really do know that TV is not real. The idea that it's just something people watch to amuse themselves isn't too much for me to comprehend. But once in a while, when something I don't expect pops up on the screen, yeah, I'll react to it.

And I'm not reacting for the amusement of my People.

If there's a fricking huge kitty on TV, I'm going to run across the room to check it out. And I might get up on my back legs for a good look.

But that doesn't mean I want anyone to laugh at me.

In fact, the next time one of them laughs, I'm going to find whatever food they're munching on, and spit on it. Or worse.

SEPTEMBER 3, 2004

What is it with people and pork?

Look, if you don't know if kitties can have pork, *find out*.
Pick up the phone, call the kitty doctor.
And then give me some of the damned ham already!

SEPTEMBER 4, 2004

I'm trying to figure out the point of the Woman's recent flurry of activity. There used to be all these boxes in my private little litter box room, and since they didn't keep me from what I needed to do in there, I didn't mind them. But now she's taking the boxes out, to another room, where she picks through them, as if she doesn't know what's in there.

Hello? Does she not remember that she's the one who put that stuff in those boxes?

It's harmless enough, and it keeps her occupied so that she's not bugging me, but she's not leaving any boxes empty for me! I don't ask for much, and I did notice the other day that my see-through box seems to be missing...so why won't she leave just *one* of those boxes empty for me? And what is so freaking important about looking in them anyway? If she'd listen I could tell her— nothing important. If there were food in any of them, it'd be bad by now anyway.

I dunno...this just doesn't seem like it's a good thing, at least not for me.

SEPTEMBER 5, 2004

There are only 3 things you need to keep your cat happy:

1.   Food on demand
2.   A clean litter box on demand
3.   Treats on demand

Now, anything else is just gravy—and gravy is nice, too, especially if it's just a little bit warm and not terribly lumpy—but most cats will be perfectly happy with those 3 things. Well, kitty crack once in a while is nice. And back scratches with just the very tips of your fingers. A nice fuzzy blanket would be most welcome, too, come to think of it. But you have to admit, those are 3 very important things.

Oh, and bow to your cat once in a while. We know we deserve it.

SEPTEMBER 6, 2004

The bowl was on the counter.
The macaroni and cheese was in the bowl.
The Woman left the room.
Anything on the counter is mine, we've established that.

So why did she get all bent when she came back and I was licking the macaroni and cheese? It's not like I ate any. I only licked off a little bit of cheese, not even enough to matter. Certainly not enough to warrant throwing all of it away.

But it was quite tasty, I'll give her that.

SEPTEMBER 7, 2004

There was a bottle cap on the floor, and the Man stepped on it.
Somehow, that was my fault.

Did I put it there?

Well…yeah. But I'm not the one who left it on the table for a kitty to play with, now, am I?

Your bottle cap.
Your foot.
Not my problem.

SEPTEMBER 8, 2004

Oooh yeah.
I've been dumped off the Woman's lap eight times tonight for being an annoy-ing pest.
I think that's a record or something.

SEPTEMBER 9, 2004

Well here's something I don't recommend:

If you feel like sticking your face close your Human's—for whatever reason, be it nuzzles or nibbles—make sure they're not about to sneeze.

That is really, really unpleasant.

SEPTEMBER 10, 2004

Human armpits can be quite tasty, but for some reason, people don't seem to enjoy having them licked.

SEPTEMBER 11, 2004

They took me outside! ALL THE WAY OUTSIDE!!! LOOK!

I mean, come on! Not only did they shove me inside that plastic tomb, but they took me outside where all the sticky little creatures were playing. LOOK! They stuck their fingers in to try to touch me, they laughed, they were loud, and little littlest one...oh crap, he actually banged on it!

Worse yet, I could smell food on their germy little hands, but did I get any? Was there a reward for me not biting their dirty little fingers off?

Hell no! I just had to sit there and take it for like FIVE MINUTES!

Surely, this is poop-on-the pillow worthy.

SEPTEMBER *12, 2004*

It's only taken 3 years, but I think I finally have the Woman trained. Every morning, after she uses the giant litter box and changes her clothes, she makes the giant bed for me, smoothing out my giant fuzzy cat blanket, so I can spread out and take a nice, long nap. She used to wait for a good hour or two before making the bed (if she ever did...I remember days on end where she was too lazy to just pull the covers up and smooth everything out...) but now she gets right to it.

Now, sure, I'd be happier if she'd do that first thing, but I understand having to use the litter box. And she might as well change clothes while she's in the bathroom. Oh, and she swallows a pill while she's in there, too, and I gather it's important, so I don't mind that delay much, either...as long as she makes the bed for me before she leaves the bedroom.

Persistence pays off, I suppose. Which makes me think that I need to keep on them about feeding me on demand. Sooner or later they're just going to cave in.

SEPTEMBER *13, 2004*

People.
You are not my Owners.
You are my Staff.

I thought that was apparent...

SEPTEMBER 14, 2004

Human food should not come in containers that sounds like cat food when opened.
Really, it shouldn't.
That sound is a tease, and it's not fair.

SEPTEMBER 15, 2004

My stuff is going missing, and I don't like it one bit. First the nice loveseat upon which I occasionally napped suddenly vanished, and today it's the piano. And not just that, the bench I sat on to look out the front door went with it. The Woman keeps going through things and throwing or giving stuff away... I'm afraid if I'm not careful, my bed will be next. Or worse, *me!*

This just isn't right. And I have the feeling things are only going to get worse...

SEPTEMBER 16, 2004

Kitty crack, kitty crack, kitty kitty kitty crack…

SEPTEMBER 17, 2004

The plastic thingy on the desk might not *need* teeth marks in.
But now it *has* teeth marks in it.
So why comment about it now?
I should have been told that first.
Right?

SEPTEMBER 18, 2004

You know that thingy that people often put to their ear and then talk into?
It should *not* be allowed to make noise when a kitty is lying right next to it.

SEPTEMBER 19, 2004

Just because I lay like a lump on the hall floor, or I don't come running when you come in the front door, it doesn't mean I don't feel well.

It means I'm pissed off at you, I just felt like chillin' in the hallway, I'm sound asleep, or I'm pissed off at you. Maybe even ticked.

But it doesn't mean I'm sick. Not even if I barf in the closet.

SEPTEMBER 20, 2004

They took me outside again. Not only did I have to put up with the Sticky People, but the Man kept running a stick over the plastic tomb, and also kept sticking it through the slats at me. What the hell is wrong with these people? I'm not a fricking *dog* that has to be let out everyday because he's too stupid to use a litter box. I'm a *cat*, People, a *feline*. I'm perfectly all right with staying inside where it's safe and quiet.

When the Woman took me back inside and opened the door to my tomb, I bit her.

Yeah, I said it. *I bit her.* And she deserved it. I bet she won't be doing *that* for a while now, eh?

SEPTEMBER 21, 2004

I'm not real sure I understand why some kitties prefer to play outside…I watch them from my window, and while they have a whole lot of space, they're awfully far away from their food dish and litter box, not to mention all the Sticky People there are outside. And the cars. Holy crap, people zoom down the street so freaking fast—a cat could get squished before he could blink.

I *sometimes* kind of like going outside if I'm in the plastic tomb—if there are no people around. Or at least quiet people. I like the feel of the wind and I like being able to watch things, but there's no way I want to be out there unprotected. And trust me, People are no real protection. Something starts to happen and their voices get all high pitched and whiny, and their brains just fall out. They get really stupid and don't know what to do.

It's definitely safer inside, or in the plastic tomb. A cat can see it all from there, and not have to worry about being carted off by a giant squirrel. Or a Sticky Creature.

SEPTEMBER 22, 2004

Any discussion that begins with "We need to talk about your bathroom habits" is bound to be one sided. Yeah. One sided. I am not going to sit here and listen to the criticisms of the naturally occurring effects of having a digestive system.

Look, people, *you* try using a litter box. Give up the big white throne litter box and use the real one. Let's see how well *you* do trying to squat in a little box of sand and have perfect aim. Let's see how well *you* keep the litter in the box. Go ahead. Try it.

Oh, but first, tape fur to your feet. Then try to get out of the box without leaving a little bit of litter trailing behind you. And let's not forget the important act of burying your waste—come on, face it. The box is not the biggest thing in the world, the litter gets wet, so yeah, once in a while some is going to fly out and stick to the wall. Deal with it!

Your world is not going to come to an end if you have to sweep stray litter up once in a while, and your fingers will not fall off if you occasionally have to pick up a piece of poop that didn't quite make it into the box.

And if you try to have this little talk with me again, I'm going to start using the bathtub instead. Let's see how you like cleaning *that* up.

SEPTEMBER 23, 2004

When the man in the brown truck brings a box, it's not fair to just set it down and not open it. Open the box! Come on already! I don't care if you already know what's in it, open the box already! *I want the freaking box!*

SEPTEMBER 24, 2004

Tonight I decided to wait and see if the people really pay attention to what time it is, and did not remind them that they have a hungry kitty who relies on their damned opposable thumbs. I sat quietly, just waiting.

Just as I thought—without my reminders, there would be no dinner.

Twenty minutes late, the Woman looks up and says thoughtfully, "You must be hungry by now."

Well DUH!

They need to stop complaining about my reminders, because they obviously *need* them!

SEPTEMBER 25, 2004

I smelled meat on the Woman's breath this afternoon. It was obviously meat she didn't cook at home, because I would have noticed that, and asked for a small taste. Sneaking out to have meat is just wrong, especially if you don't bring any home for the kitty.

Whatever "fajitas" are, they smell pretty damned good, even though she said they'd upset my tummy.

Yeah, whatever.

Upset the tummy and I can barf that sucker right up.
And she *didn't* say they'd make flames shoot out my ass.
I can deal with throwing up.
Why can't she?

SEPTEMBER 26, 2004

My bed. Mine. Mine mine mine mine mine.

SEPTEMBER 27, 2004

The Man likes to use this hook and yarn to make things. Right now he's making a blanket (I hope it's for me, because the yarn is soft and warm) and I keep trying to help him, but he's not very appreciative. He complains about my fur getting mixed in with the yarn (I would think that would help; you know, add a little fluff and warmth to it), he complains about me grabbing the hook (I'm just guiding it, that's all), and he complains that I'm taking up too much space on his lap, leaving him little room to work.

Look, all I'm trying to do is help. Well, that and make sure he doesn't poke my eye out with that thing. And be sure enough of my fur is involved that he gives me the blanket when he's done, just because no one else will want it.

It's pretty colors, too. My black and white fur can only make it better.

SEPTEMBER 28, 2004

Ok, so she *finally* opened the damn box. And you know what was in it?

Another freaking plastic tomb! Something else she can haul me outside in, so the sticky people can try to touch me and scream at me. Why the hell does anyone need *two* of those things???

SEPTEMBER 29, 2004

Oy. Sometimes a guys just wants to be alone, you know?

SEPTEMBER 30, 2004

There was a long skinny bug walking along the baseboard this afternoon; I was stretched out on the floor and the Woman was in the comfy chair. She looked over at it and then at me and said, "You can get that, you know."

Well, yeah.
I could.
But why would I want to?

There were no long legs to rip off, and it didn't have any wings, so why waste the energy?

It wasn't even a question worth addressing, so I rolled up a little bit and started to lick myself.

OCTOBER 1, 2004

Something to ponder.
Why would the People eat food they don't like?

Tonight the Woman cooked something meaty that even I really didn't want. It smelled funny, like old feet or something, but they sat down and ate it anyway. I could tell they weren't very happy about it because they both made faces, but the Woman said the meat wasn't *bad*, it just didn't taste very good.

So they ate it.
You can be sure I wouldn't eat something I didn't like.
Good thing for me, there's not too many things I don't like.

> There once was a cat who loved fish
> He ate it from a large dish
> He was heard once to say
> Oh I love it this way
> And to have it each day was his wish.
>
> More superb poetry by Max.

OCTOBER 2, 2004

I did *not* think that those little holes in the wall were bugs. No matter what *she* says, I absolutely did not. I only jumped up to see how deep they were. I mean, come on. For all I know there are edible things lurking in those holes.

The Man took a bunch of his shiny things off the walls, and left the holes. The shiny things looked better, if you ask me. But no one has, like my opinion on the decor of this house doesn't matter.

And the Woman tells me things are coming off the walls because we're "moving." The only moving I'm doing is from the comfy chair in the living room to the kitchen and back, with occasional side trips to the litter box. And I've been watching the Woman. She's *barely* moving at all most of the time, so I don't know what the hell she figures is really going on.

And, oh yeah, she left this morning without feeding me! I was good; I didn't launch off my window perch onto her stomach this morning. I didn't howl in her ear. I waited patiently, and instead of feeding me after she got up, she left the freaking house for half an hour! My breakfast was late. After all that being good, it was late.

I tell you what, when dinner time rolls around she better be moving her ass from where ever she's plastered to into the kitchen. That's the only moving I want to see around here.

One thing the Man gets that the Woman does not—he knows when I want to play Chase Me. Yeah, I know, it's a stupid game, but when I have so much energy I feel like I'm going to pop, it's fun. I let my hair stand on end, he hisses at me and I take off, and he follows. Sometimes he corners me, but he doesn't try to pick me up; he just makes this really stupid face, lifts his arms up high, and hisses again—and off I go.

I kind of wish I had a camera in my collar to capture that look. I think I could get blackmail money for it.

Anyway…he knows how to play that game, but the Woman is good at knowing where to scratch. Not on herself (though she seems adept at that as well; I just don't care to watch,) but she's really good at getting under my collar and under my chin. And when my back is all itchy, she takes those blunt people claws and carefully goes up and down my spine (but for some reason she keeps bringing up the subject of brushing, saying brushing would make the itchiness go away. Yeah, well, she can brush her own damn fur and itchy stuff away, I'm not having any of it.)

For people, they have their usefulness.
I just wish they would get the feeding thing down pat.
I shouldn't have to remind them every single day that I'm starving to death.

OCTOBER 4, 2004

There is *nothing* better than a basket of nice warm white clothes fresh out of the dryer. Those are the most perfect for climbing on and rolling around in, then snuggling down for a nice nap.

For some reason, the Woman always has a few choice words to say about it, but I don't think she's ever tried it.

She really should.
She's *always* cold.
It would warm her up pretty quick.

OCTOBER 5, 2004

No, I do *not* want to drink out of the toilet.
I've seen what you do in there.
I only wanted to watch the water swirl.

Sheesh. Just…gross.

OCTOBER 6, 2004

There are *people* in my house! Strange people that I don't know, and they're taking all my stuff and putting it into boxes! Worse yet, MY People seem to be okay with it—so okay that they took all my window perches down. I can't even look out the freaking window now!

Normally a bunch of boxes would be a good thing, stuff to play in and jump on, but I don't like this, not one bit. It's not quiet enough in here, I don't know where my stuff is, there's all this other stuff more or less blocking my litter box, and I don't know what the hell is going on!

I am not a happy cat today, not at all.

OCTOBER 7, 2004

Luckily, there were no strange people in my house today, but all my stuff is still in boxes, and they taped the boxes shut so that I can't get to any of it. And my People don't seem to grasp that…it's MY stuff! I want it!

The one good thing about all those boxes is that there's something to jump around on, and I'm not even getting yelled at for it. I jumped up and the hopped over on top of the big stand they have their TV on, and no one got mad. I took up all of the space on the Woman's chair, and she didn't make me move, she sat on the footstool instead.

The Woman took me outside in the new plastic tomb today, too. I hate to admit it, I kind of liked being out there. It was breezy and there were birds (but they didn't come too close) and the Peoples' friends came outside, but didn't pester me. Even the Sticky Little ones were tolerable. One of the littlest little ones called me "KiKi." I don't know who KiKi is, but she was cute, so it's okay. She didn't scream at me or stick her fingers in to poke at me, so I suppose she can call me anything she wants.

But I want my stuff back. I think my kitty crack is in one of those boxes.

October 8, 2004

We were robbed.

Seriously. EVERYTHING is gone, except for my plastic tomb and a few other odds and ends. They freaking locked me in the bathroom this morning—for the entire damned day—and when I got out late in the afternoon, it was all gone. All the boxes, my Supreme Commander Kitty Tower, the comfy chair…all gone.

And you know what? I bet the People spent all their time sitting outside on their asses so they weren't in the house to put a stop to the thievery. If they would just stay inside for ten minutes, crap like this wouldn't happen and I would have all my stuff!

They better buy me new stuff. And I mean it!

October 9, 2004

All I can do is hide…

October 11, 2004

Oh of all things holy and furry… You are NOT going to believe the crap I've gone through the last few days.

Okay, you know it started with my People letting total strangers in the house, then when I was locked in the bathroom we were robbed. Everything was gone, and I mean everything. The house was so empty that my sweet little voice echoed off the walls like a toddler screaming. Really. It was *that* empty.

So over the last couple of days the Woman started cleaning. Like, why couldn't she do that when the stuff was there? Really…everything we owned was gone, so why bother? Who cares if the house is clean now? Yesterday I was so fed up I hid up on top of the refrigerator, at one point prompting the Woman to run through the house squealing, "I can't find the cat! I can't find the cat!"

Heh. Remember that, boys and girls. It's totally worth seeing the look and hearing the squeal in their pathetic little voices.

But then they left me alone for most of the day, in that empty house. All my toys were gone, my bed was gone…all I had was a tiny little bit of food and a litter box. After a few hours of this I looked out and could finally see them outside the window, with all those other People, and they were freaking playing with *fire*. They had this circle thing filled with fire, and they were sitting around it. Don't they know that's just *wrong*?

But…it gets worse.

After they were done playing with fire, they scooped me up, shoved me into the plastic tomb—which was in their car—and took me to a strange new place. My bed was there, and my food, but none of my other stuff. We stayed there for one night, then back into the tomb I went… *for whole damned day!*

I kid you not! We made a quick stop home—the house was still empty—and my People stood in the yard hugging all the other people (yeah, gag me)…and then we left.

All.

Damned.

Day.

So now we're in another strange room (I have to admit it's nicer than the last one) and they let me out of the tomb, but I think I can kiss off ever seeing my stuff again.

This is *so* poop on the pillow worthy…

OCTOBER 12, 2004

I think I figured out what "moving" *really* means.

It doesn't mean getting from one side of the room to the other, or turning 3 or 4 times to soften your bed pillows. It means being shoved into this plastic tomb, put in the car, where you stay All Freaking Day. Not just for a little while, but from sunup until it's dark. The people get out every once in a while, but every time I try they tell me no, I have to stay, they'll let me out "later."

And I tell you what—those plastic tombs are impossible to dig one's way out of.

I may have figured something else out today. Instead of talking to them all day—and yeah, I did that yesterday, thinking that if I asked politely they would take me home—I just curled up after a couple of hours and went to sleep. Since I'm well rested, tonight while they try to sleep, I'm going to run around the room at top speed, howling my head off.

That'll teach 'em.

OCTOBER 13, 2004

It works!

If you sleep all day, you have all night to drive your People NUTS. I let them sleep a little last night, but at about 5 a.m., I started. It was awesome. I jumped on them, I practically danced all over the bed, I head butted and rubbed on them…

And it got them up, when it was still dark outside.

Yeah, sure, they stuffed me back into that tomb and I spent the next 14 freaking hours in the car, but they fed me well, and now we're in another room. I expect it'll be the same tomorrow, hour after hour after hour in that car…

=sigh=
This is my life now, isn't it?

OCTOBER 15, 2004

Man, they did it to me again yesterday…we got up and they shoved me into the tomb and back into the car. I complained enough—and loudly, very loudly—that they stopped early and I got to relax the rest of the day.

And I must have been really annoying, because this morning they left me alone. They've been in and out, but I get to stay here, curled up on the bed or in a chair. I don't particularly like this place because there's not enough room, but if it means not getting back in that car, it'll do.

OCTOBER 16, 2004

The Younger Human!!! They brought me to see the Younger Human!!! He and his Much Better Smelling Friend showed up at that little room we were in, and talked to me and petted me. Of course, I couldn't let them know how happy I was to see them, but hell! Now I know why we had to spend so much time in the freaking car!

Yesterday they didn't make me ride in it, but today they did. This morning the Woman put me in the tomb and took me to the car, but I was only in it for about 10 minutes. They drove me to a new place, a much, much bigger place than that room. It smells funny, but there's a lot to explore. And the Woman keeps saying "no more rides, you're safe," but I don't believe her.

But it's a nice place, so maybe…

OCTOBER 17, 2004

I most certainly was NOT admiring myself in the bathroom mirror. I just happened to be lounging there on the vanity, looked over my shoulder, and realized that I could see myself. I was not lost in my absolute beauty (though one could understand how that could happen); I simply was surprised and continued to look to make sure that it really was me and not some random kitty trash that might have wandered, uninvited, into the new house.

OCTOBER 18, 2004

I heard the People talking about hamsters today. I wasn't clear on whether they meant *they* want hamsters, or the Younger Human wants hamsters, but they were definitely talking about hamsters in the sense that someone wants a pair of dwarf hamsters as pets.

People.
Hamsters are not pets.
Hamsters are a Main Course.

Well, the dwarf variety, they're more like an appetizer…

OCTOBER 19, 2004

The people just got back from buying food, but I watched as they put it all away, and there was *nothing* there for me. Not one damned thing. It was all people food, and not very healthy food at that.

So what am I supposed to do for sustenance?

I am so totally not eating bugs…

OCTOBER 20, 2004

I am going to sit in the Woman's office and stare at her until she feeds me.

She doesn't seem to like that very much. After about five minutes she scowls and says "What?" and then her concentration is broken and she can't work anymore.

If I keep staring, she'll get up, and if she gets up, she might as well feed me!

OCTOBER 21, 2004

There's not a whole lot you can do when your people are sad, other than crawling up on their laps and nuzzling their faces.

OCTOBER 22, 2004

Ok, boys and girls, this is the true definition of "Moving" :

First, you will be locked in a bathroom, during which time everything you own and love will disappear.

Then, you will spend 2 days in an empty house, your sad and confused meows echoing off the walls. Right at the point when you think maybe your people just went broke and had to sell it all, they shove you in this *tomb* and then into the car, where you will spend the next 4 days, all freaking day long, with nightly breaks to stay in strange and awful-smelling rooms.

If you're lucky, at the end of the 4 days you get to stay in one of those rooms for more than one night, and your Younger Human will show up. But *then* you'll be tossed back into the tomb and the car and taken to another strange new place. It's bigger, but it's still different. And no stuff.

After 3 or 4 days of that, you'll start to relax. Once you relax they grab you and throw you into another bathroom for an entire day. It'll be hot in that bathroom, so you have to howl a lot to make sure they know you're pissed about it. But when you come out—Boxes and Boxes and Boxes, all there to jump on and climb on, and most of it smells like your stuff, even though you can't see your stuff. Your stuff will be somewhere in those boxes, and you just have to get really bitchy about it, complaining until the People rescue it all for you.

But that's moving.
I don't recommend it.

~~~

We need a screen on the front door. I would like to look out it, like I did in the old house, but this one doesn't have one. If they leave the front door open, bugs get in, and no one wants the bugs (especially me, because they would expect me to chase them, catch them, and eat them, and I just don't do that.) They point out that I could get out, but I don't have any strong wish to go outside here. There are too many other cats out there, and they're not very nice. I sit in the window and say hello, but none of them even reply.

Well, there is a female cat who seems really friendly, but she wants something I just don't have anymore.

Really, I just want to lay in front of the door on the cool tile, and look outside. Is a screen too much to ask for?

Obviously it is…they keep saying we can't have one because the apartment won't allow it. Well hell, don't ask the apartment. I give you permission!

October 23, 2004

It just occurred to me—I haven't seen any of the Sticky Little People in a long time. I did see another cat outside a window, and I tried to talk to him, but he just looked at me like I was speaking some foreign language. I think the People forgot to bring the Sticky Ones along…

October 24, 2004

I heard a new Sticky Person outside today squealing, "I three years old, I three years old."
Guess what, kid? So I am.
Big freaking deal.

October 25, 2004

Heh.

Evidently, there's another cat around here who looks a lot like me. This is funny only because when the People came home today, the first thing they did was start calling my name (no, I didn't answer…why would I?) and looking into rooms and closets to find me. This was even funnier, because I was right there in the living room, in front of the door, lounging on the sofa, and neither of them noticed me.

After a few minutes of this, with the Woman muttering, "That couldn't have been him, that couldn't have been him," they headed toward the front door, when I decided to yawn loudly. Not that I wanted to make their search any easier, but I did feel the need to yawn, and what the hell…maybe a treat would come out of it.

She turned around sharply and snapped "Why didn't you answer us?"

Well, duh, because you wanted me to.

"We thought you'd gotten outside!!"

So this explains why you were looking for me *inside*.

"Dammit, you blend into that black sofa. Do you want a treat? Is the kitty hungry?"

Score.

OCTOBER 26, 2004

Before we moved, the Woman gave me a peanut to play with. Now I have to admit, when she first put it on the floor I looked at her like she was insane, but after I batted it around a little bit I realized this could be a lot of fun. Plus, it smelled pretty good.

I'd forgotten about that until just a few minutes ago, when she looked at me and said "You know, when we were cleaning the other house, I don't remember ever finding that peanut I gave you to play with."

Well…yeah.

She thinks it's in a box somewhere, rotting.
I think it's fertilizer somewhere, having long passed through my digestive system.
I should show her an example of where it might be.

OCTOBER 27, 2004

I wish we still had stairs. I miss the sound of my feet thundering on the wood when I'd run down them at full tilt. But right now I miss them because I have this terrific plastic bottle cap, and no stairs to throw it down. And I would have saved the throwing until 3 a.m., when I'd have lots of peace and quiet to make all my noise.

OCTOBER 28, 2004

All of this "moving" might actually work to my benefit. So far I have 2 *huge* beds to pick from for my napping needs, plus the Woman has her comfy chair for me to lounge on.

In one room there's my tower, and it's right next to the bookcases, which I can climb on. In the kitchen I seem to be allowed on the counters, and the Woman says when she puts away the stuff she has on top of the cupboards I'll be allowed to play up there, too.

The downside is that I have to share a bathroom with the Woman—no more private litter box room—and there don't seem to be any Sticky Little People around here. But there are other cats outside, an though they won't talk to me yet, I think they might soon. The Woman said one of them tried to come inside the other day, and what other reason would he have than to come see me?

I'll be glad when all the boxes are gone. They were fun for a while, but I'd rather they just get the rest of my stuff out of the boxes. I want my stuff.

OCTOBER 29, 2004

This afternoon the Woman picked me up and took me outside. Without the plastic tomb. But you know what? It was no big freaking deal. This new place doesn't have a front yard with a tree and Sticky People running around. It has cement. And cement is nothing worth looking at.

I think she agreed, because we were only out there for a minute. You know it sucks when a minute is all you can take of the Great Outdoors.

We need a tree out there. Or at least something tall enough that I can see over the patio wall.

OCTOBER 30, 2004

How old do you have to be to vote? Because I want to vote on a law that requires the doubling of the size of cans of Stinky Goodness.

OCTOBER 31, 2004

In this new place we live, some of the people have places to live that are higher up than ours, and they have these outside things they can sit on (after a check, they're called "balconies.") Some of those people have pets, too, and I don't think the pets are very happy. Just this morning I was looking out, and there was a dog on one of the balconies, and he was standing on his back legs, looking down below.

I yelled "*jump!*" a few times, but I don't think he heard me.

NOVEMBER 1, 2004

The People were in and out all day; I was napping most of the time so I didn't really care, but when they came home the last time they both smelled a lot like the Younger Human.

They saw him and didn't take me! Worse yet, they didn't bring him home!

Cheap bastards, you just know they didn't bring him home because they would have had to feed him. And we all know what tight asses they can be about that.

NOVEMBER 2, 2004

We're back to this stupid time change thing again. People, really, why do you keep screwing around with your clocks? It makes you sleep in late, which in turn means my stomach is *growling* for an extra hour, and it means I get my dinner later than I should.

Give it up already! Just pick a time and stick with it, and all your kitties will be happy.

Well, happy provided you get your ample behinds out of bed at a reasonable time to open our cans of Stinky Goodness.

Consider the importance of a well fed cat.
And poopless pillows.

NOVEMBER 3, 2004

I keep trying to talk to the cats that are wandering around outside, but they're rude and never respond. So today, while it's raining, I take great pleasure in standing by the window and shouting out, "Hey you! Ha! I'm dry and you're not! Phffft."

I don't always have to be mature.

~ ~ ~

I can hear Sticky People outside, but I can't see them. The window I was sitting at doesn't have a very good view of the world; half if it is blocked by the building and the other half is blocked by the dumbest looking bush I've ever seen. I kind of want to see if they're the right Sticky People, but even when I went to another window I couldn't tell.

I heard some older Humans, too, but I know those weren't the right humans. These were yelling at the Sticky People, and the right humans never did that, at least not with bad words. And trust me, I know bad words when I hear them.

Not because I ever *say* them… but I know them.

I'm waiting for one of the Sticky People to say those words back. That might be fun.

November 4, 2004

The Younger Human and his Better Smelling Friend were here tonight, but I only know this because I can smell them on the furniture. I was asleep when they got here—did it not occur to either of the People that I might want to *see* them? There are 2 people in this world who treat me the way a kitty should be treated—they'll play with me but they won't insinuate themselves on me—but I slept right through it. Because *they* didn't want me to have any fun. There can't be any other reason that they didn't wake me up. They just don't want me to have any fun.

November 5, 2004

Conversation with the Woman:

Me: I'm hungry.
Her: *unintelligible mumblings.*
Me: Just feed me!
Her: *unintelligible mumblings.*
Me: Come on, I'm starving.
Her: *unintelligible mumblings.*
Me: You would stuff your face without a second thought if you were hungry.

Her: *unintelligible mumblings.*
Me: Please?
Her: Bite me.
Me: Bitch.

NOVEMBER 6, 2004

I think I broke the Woman.

She was on the new sofa, lying on her side, watching TV, and I was in the kitchen on the counter... Seriously, I didn't know she was there, and I sailed over the high part of the counter into the living room, and landed kind of on her hip and butt. And I know it hurt because she didn't yell at me, she just made this gross sucking sound and grabbed her side.

If I had known she was there, I would have aimed for her boobs.
Lots more padding there.

NOVEMBER 7, 2004

Now that we're in California, it occurred to me that I should learn a little Spanish. Mostly I just want to be able to understand *Telemundo*, but it could come in handy every now and then. So with some determination and careful study of the numerous Spanish speaking TV channels, I have learned the *most* important thing I need to be able to say.

Yo quiero Stinky Goodness.

I'm working on "Go to work so you can buy me Stinky Goodness."

There's a girl cat outside and she's howling her little fool head off. I *know* what she wants, and I keep telling her I can't help her because my People had my nads cut off, but she's so busy yowling I don't think she heard me.

There are other cats around so I'm sure she'll get herself something...but dammit, why did the people have my goodies removed? This was a chance to meet other cats and have a good time!

Unless she's a slutty cat of course. I just thought of that.
There's not a whole lot worse than cat slut.
I know that, because I watch Animal Planet.

Um, yeah, I *do* think that if I press hard enough with the top of my head, your boobs will invert and create more space for me when I sit on your lap. Deal with it!

~ ~ ~

What difference does it make if I get up on the counter when you're making a sandwich or not? You do realize that I get up on the counter all the time, right? And when I get up there, I run my butt alllll over it. Back and forth, up and down…So does it really matter if I jump up while you're slathering mustard on a piece of bread? Does it?

~ ~ ~

The blinds were open on the windows today, so I had high hopes of getting a really good sunspot to nap in. It's one of the few true joys in life that a cat has—finding the warmest place in the house and curling up there to snooze the day away.

But there was no sunspot. And it occurs to me that I don't think I've seen one in this new place.

There's another bad thing about moving—they left the freaking sunspots back at the other place!

I bet those Sticky Little People are hogging them, too.

~ ~ ~

There's a dog in the next building that stands out on the balcony and yaps its little head off. The yapping is the only way anyone can tell it's a dog…this thing is about half my size and doesn't seem to have much fur, but it's got freakishly huge ears. It's like a nervous, barking rat.

I don't think its people know that it's so small it could squeeze between the balcony rails and fall to the ground.

I'm not telling them.

~ ~ ~

I saw some Sticky People today.

I was sitting in the Woman's office, on the window seat the Man finally put up for me, and saw three or four of them outside playing with some sort of large ball.

They weren't Sticky LITTLE People—I'd say these were medium sized people—but there was definitely something sticky about them.

I think those might be what the Woman calls "Pre-teens."
It sounds like they can only get worse before they get better.
Makes me glad I'm in here and not out there where they can get hold of me.

November 9, 2004

So, the Woman thinks the odors emanating from my litter box are offensive. Her solution? A couple of big cinnamon scented candles. And you know what it smells like in the bathroom after those have been lit for a couple of hours? Cinnamon scented cat shit. Yep. That'll help.

~~~

The Man is growing fur on his face.
I hate to tell him, but it's not going to help him look more like me.
The white in *my* fur is *supposed* to be there…

November 11, 2004

I just wanted to take a minute to say Thank You to all the men and women who, throughout the generations, have served in the military, protecting my rights as a cat, enabling me to be the consumer of cans of Stinky Goodness, instead of being the cans' contents. 'Cause, in some places, that can happen, you know.

~~~

Something is missing from this new place; it took me a while to figure it out, but last night when the People were asleep and I was feeling a little bit chilly, it hit me.

Those things near the floor that blow warm air…there are none here. That was one of the things I enjoyed the most when it was cold—being able to curl up in front of the one that was in the bathroom or the one my bed was in front of.

So I did a little exploring, and I think I know where they are here—by the freaking ceiling!

WTF?

People, they do *no good* being near the ceiling. A kitty just cannot get up that high, nor is there anything to curl upon. And from surfing around online, I now know that heat rises, so *come on!* Those warm air thingies should be near the floor where a kitty can enjoy them, and where they make more sense. After all, people get cold too, and if the warm air is up at the ceiling, their nipples are going to invert just as much as mine will.

NOVEMBER 12, 2004

It's still kind of early and the Woman is ~~drinking vodka right from the bottle~~ hard at work on the other computer, writing her next best seller, but I'm bored.

I don't get bored very often. My days are usually quite full: get the Woman up, eat, use the litter box, take a nap, get up, look out the window, beg for treats, nap, get up, jump on her lap and nap, wake up, stretch, try to convince her it's dinner time, use the litter box, nap, get up, bitch at her because it IS dinner time, eat, nap, bathe, nap, get up, beg for treats, look out the window, nap…

You can see where I just don't have time to get bored.

But today, I'm a little bored. There's nothing really to see outside the window, and the Woman is useless when she's ~~drinking~~ working.

I'd even settle for watching TV, but I can't get the remote control to work, and the Woman doesn't seem to understand when I ask her to turn it on for me.

It's just a sad, sad day.
I suppose I'll just go nap.

NOVEMBER 13, 2004

Ever since that stupid time change, the Woman just doesn't seem able to get out of bed early enough. I'm a *very* good kitty and I wait patiently until 8 o'clock, but she's still lying there like a lump, drooling onto her pillow.

I've tried being nice about waking her up, but then she complains about me getting hair up her nose or in her mouth. If she would just get up, this wouldn't be a problem!

I hate the damned time change. That's what the problem is. The stupid time change. She was fine before that. Now she stays up late ~~drinking~~ watching TV or working, and then she can't get herself up at a decent hour.

One of these mornings she's going to get up and find me curled up in a ball on the floor, in a hypoglycemic stupor. I might even froth at the mouth and have seizures. *Then* she'll feel bad.

She better feel bad.

NOVEMBER 14, 2004

The Man got up this morning and left the house; I thought maybe he was finally going off to the place where he's going to pass gas, but he was only gone for a few hours, so I guess not.

But after he left, I went to see if the Woman was ready to get up. Apparently not. I barely took two steps into the room and barely got my mouth open, when she reached for a pillow and aimed it at me. She didn't even open her eyes! She just reached and looked like she was going to throw it, but luckily she just dropped her arm and let it go.

Since she obviously wasn't getting up, I jumped up on the bed and made myself comfortable. On top of her. And I shifted and rearranged myself several times, because she would surely want me to be comfortable while lying smack dab in the middle of her stomach.

Well, if I were her I'd want me to be comfortable.

NOVEMBER 15, 2004

Look…I know it's a teddy bear. I've seen it on the comfy chair a hundred times. I know it's not real, it doesn't growl, it doesn't bite—it doesn't do anything at all.

But when you move it to a new place and I don't see you do it, well, yeah, I might get a bit confused, just seeing a tuft of brown fur from the corner of my eye. And knowing that the dog is long gone, I may jump to a conclusion or two. Like maybe, just maybe, you brought home a new one. Or worse yet, one found its way into the house completely uninvited.

So sure, if I see that unprepared, my fur is going to stand on end, I'm going to crouch down, and I'm going to stalk it. I'm going to slink very slowly across the floor and approach with trepidation, at the ready in case it moves. I am going to protect my territory.

But *you* don't need to sit there and watch, laughing through your nose, and you especially don't need to make a loud, obnoxious barking sound when I get within a foot.

You're lucky I didn't whiz all over your bed.

November 16, 2004

I have this giant fuzzy blanket; I know it's mine because it has a giant white cat on it (the Woman says it's a white tiger, but I'm not stupid…I *know* what a cat looks like…) I let the People keep it on the giant bed, and I even allow them to use it at night, but you'd think they'd also make space for me up there.

It really is a big bed. There's more than enough room for two people and a cat. But the Woman has to have these two really long body pillows on the bed with her—she says they keep her back from hurting too much—and they both have a couple of other pillows. I don't know why, they just do. Like drooling onto the mattress isn't good enough.

With the size of the people and the sheer volume of the pillows, there isn't always enough free bed space for a cat. So sure, I have no problem with plopping down on top of one of the People. I usually choose the Woman because even when she's asleep, she doesn't push me off. Sometimes she moans, "Oh, Max, move already," but she obviously doesn't mean it.

If she meant it she'd shove me aside, right?

So why does she then get upset that my weight has made her legs fall asleep? Or why does it bother her that some of my fur went up her nose? Why does she care that once in a while she wakes up with my ass in her face?

It's MY blanket, People. I'm being nice and SHARING. If that means a moment or two of wonderous feline ass face, deal with it.

Better yet, sleep someplace else.

The place we live now is different from the last place we lived. There aren't very many Sticky Little People around, and when they are outside, they don't stay very long. I don't know where they play, but it's not outside my window.

And there are no stairs for me to run up and down. It didn't occur to me when the People first brought me here, but now I realize there are none, and I miss that. Stairs are especially fun in the middle of the night when people are in bed but not quite asleep…scrambling up and down, as loudly as a cat can, is great fun.

I know there's an upstairs because I can hear things going on up there. So can the Woman. I was with her in the bathroom yesterday and she looked up and said quietly, "Crap, that man pees louder than God."

I don't know about that, having never heard God pee, so I'll take her word for it.

But, lady, think about this: if you heard him pee, I *know* he heard you fart. I think the whole city heard that one.

~ ~ ~

Cheap assed people.

I was sitting on the bed, looking up at the light, trying to get the Woman to turn it on. I mean, come on, just because I can see in the dark that doesn't mean I always want to BE in the dark. Once in a while it would be nice to lay there on the bed in the evening, with a light on.

First she thought I was looking at a bug, but she couldn't see one.
Then she thought I was stoned, but there was no kitty crack nearby.

Finally she realized I wanted light. And you know what she said? *Do you?* She said "No, it costs money to run the lights, and we don't need this one on."

So?
SO?

I didn't *need* it on, either. I *wanted* it on.
Don't I count?

Holy flying Pope on a pogo stick, I swear, these people are so tight they can bend quarters with their butt cheeks.

November 17, 2004

I was watching some commercial on TV and it got me to wondering… What's so wonderful about thinking outside the box?

I think outside the box.

Sometimes, I poop outside it, too.

November 18, 2004

The Woman opened the closet this afternoon and I crept in behind her…the *tomb* is in there. With a door off. And don't ask me why, but I crawled inside, and I swear I could feel the car moving under me.

So when she wasn't looking, I coughed a hairball into her shoe.
She *did* stick me in that thing during the move, after all.

November 19, 2004

Okay, so maybe it wasn't my best idea, but the Woman was sound asleep, the blankets were shoved aside, and her shirt was kind of crumpled up a bit, exposing her bare tummy.

As I sat there on the bed, wondering how she could possibly be comfortable, it occurred to me that her belly button is about the same size as my nose. Maybe a tad bigger, which means my nose could fit in it. Quite nicely.

And, well, that's how I wound up flying from the bed to the comfy chair in the corner…

November 20, 2004

Hey, if you want, I can tell you why it's called "In-N-Out Burgers."
Really, I know this one!

November 21, 2004

Oh, man, talk about *power*!

The Woman was here in her office, working, when I wandered in and meowed at her. All I was saying was "You need to comb your hair because it looks *really* bad," but she thought I wanted something.

So, she tried to figure out what it was.

She made the bed so I would have a comfy napping place.

She refilled my dry food dish—even tossing out the crumbs at the bottom so it was all fresh.

She changed my litter box. She didn't just scoop it out, she changed it all the way.

She opened the window in the office so that I could look outside (it's raining) and laugh at the dog stuck out on the balcony in the next building.

All it took was a little muttering on my part, and she did all that without any real fuss.

Damn, it's good to be a feline god.

November 22, 2004

The Man finally put up one of my special window seats today (it took him freaking long enough) and what's the first thing I see while I'm tying to relax there, soaking up some fresh air?

Some yappy little dog, yapping it's yappy little head off, annoying the entire freaking world.

Really…someone sedate those things. They're not as cute as they think they are, and they can't be used for food, so just sedate them. We'll all be happier for it.

November 23, 2004

Some days are just awesome. Today I woke up, and the Man fed me right off the bat, then the Woman got up and made the giant bed up so I could nap on the fuzzy blanket. They went somewhere for a while, and when they came back they brought two people with them.

Now, at first I was a little upset, because no one warned me there would be strange people, but after a bit I realized they smelled familiar. The man they brought looks a lot like the Man, just a little older and quite a bit cuter. They were both nice to me, paid proper homage by petting me a little and then leaving me alone, so they can come back.

Later, my tummy was growling so hard I thought I was about to turn inside out, and the People kept saying "You have two hours, Max. Dinner isn't for two hours." But then the Woman said, "Screw it, he had the gravy stuff this morning and he's probably starving."

So she fed me!
AND she says I'll get a little more tonight.
Score.

It is *so* awesome to be me most of the time.
What else could a cat want?
I have trained People!

~ ~ ~

The People were talking today about doing something called "Thanksgiving," and they're doing it at someone else's house. I'm not sure what Thanksgiving is, but if they're doing it somewhere else, it probably just means I'm getting screwed out of something good. They even mentioned calling the Younger Human and telling him that he and his Much Better Smelling Friend are invited. But no one said a word to me about it. It's not like I want to *go* anywhere, but dammit, if something fun is going on, I should at least be given the option. Especially if there's food involved.

NOVEMBER 24, 2004

From listening to conversations around the house, I've been able to pick up a few details about why the People are both always home. The Man is now "retired," though I don't see how, since it's not like he did anything to get tired in the first place. He used to pass gas (I hate to tell the Woman, but he still does) for the Air Force, and did it so long they finally told him to stop.

There have been times I wanted to tell him to stop, too, but I didn't know that was an option.

But, in a couple of weeks, he's going to pass gas for someone else. I didn't know that was allowed, either—I thought he was only really allowed to pass gas for the Woman—but she seems pretty happy about it.

Most importantly, in those discussions I've come to the conclusion that when the Man goes to pass gas for these new people, he will be able to bring home even more and better Stinky Goodness, as well as SHRIMP!

I don't know why he has to wait a couple of weeks. The Woman wants him to start now, but I suppose he has to let it build up before he can pass it.

But, I'm impressed. He passed gas for the Air Force for TWENTY years.

That's a lot of gas.

~~~

The People went out today while I was sound asleep, curled up in a comfy ball in the middle of the big furry blanket, and I didn't even realize they were gone until I heard them opening the front door.

So, upon hearing the key, I got up and wandered to the litter box, probably the same time the Woman looked into the room to see where I was.

She didn't see me on the bed, where she expected, so of course something horrible must have happened. She went looking under beds, in other rooms, everywhere except the most logical place (Hey, folks, think about what you tend to do when you first wake up. You go pee, right?)

While she was looking in the Man's computer room, he spotted me wandering into the kitchen and told her I was there...and she actually came in to see for herself (like he would lie) and then gave me some treats.

Now, I'm not complaining, but isn't giving treats to a kitty for nothing having happened kind of like the way the Air Force gives people medals for not getting lost during a move? It's nice, but not exactly necessary.

I think the Man got some of those medals.
I think my treats are better.

November 25, 2004

The People left me alone all *freaking day* today. After daintily munching my

Stinky Goodness this morning, the Younger Human came over, and they all left together. This didn't bother me too much, since it was nap time and I fully intended to nap as deeply as I possibly could, but when I woke up they were still gone.

There was more Stinky Goodness in the kitchen, but no People. So I ate it, bathed, and went back to bed, but when I woke up, still no People.

Dinner time came and went, and still they were not home. If not for the Magical Stinky Goodness Fairy, I would have starved to death before they managed to drag their sorry asses back from where ever they went.

They finally showed up three and a half damned hours after my dinner time— and they smelled like DOG. Not just that, but turkey, too.

I can get over the injustice of them whoring around with some dog for a little while—been there, done that—but they had TURKEY.

WITHOUT ME!

Oh, they offered me more Stinky Goodness and a bite of ham, but I showed them. I only ate the Stinky Goodness, and left the ham on the kitchen floor, so that one of them might step onto it with their bare feet.

I wish I had a hairball brewing, so I could hock it up into someone's brand new shoes.

November 26, 2004

I hit the farking mother load! A can of Stinky Goodness with *huge* pieces of shrimp in it. Usually when I get that flavor there are tiny chopped up pieces, but this can had 3 or 4 good sized pieces of shrimpy wonder, and the Woman let me have all of them at once. Oh holy crap, I think I am going to die right now.

Well, maybe not *die*. Not right this very moment. Because thinking about it, there are some even bigger shrimp in the freezer, and I intend to get my paws on them one way or another.

The Woman says those are for the Younger Human's Much Better Smelling

Friend when they come over for dinner sometime soon, but I'm not sure I can wait that long. Because in people terms, "sometime soon" could be as long as 4 or 5 days, and I don't think I could stand that.

NOVEMBER 27, 2004

Some mornings the Man is the one who gets up and opens my can of Stinky Goodness; I don't really care who does it, as long as it's done in a timely manner, before the growling in my tummy makes me nauseous.

However.

After I've eaten, I'm a little sleepy and want to lie down and take a nap. And my preferred napping spot after eating is the big bed with MY fuzzy blanket. So, of course, I have to work hard at getting the Woman to get out of the bed, and to get her to smooth the sheets and blankets out for me.

It is the least she could do, considering I allow her to use my fuzzy blanket in the first place.

But does she appreciate this? No! She seems to think that since I've had my breakfast, I should be happy and content, and most of all, quiet. Well. Psycho Kitty don't play that game. I feel perfectly justified in standing just out of reach, calling to her over and over and over, until she finally gets her ample ass out of my bed.

This morning…holy crap. This morning she threatened me with bodily harm. I'm serious! I stood by the bedroom door, calling out to her (loud enough to wake her up, yes) and she said if I didn't shut up, she would throw something at me.

The nerve!

And no, I didn't shut up. I called out even louder, until she did exactly what I wanted. She got up. And after she got dressed, she made the bed.

All for me.
I win.

The People bought this sofa when we moved into the new place…they said they wanted extra seating for when other People come over (like the Younger Human, I think), but mostly I think they just wanted to be able to stretch out and be lazy when they watch TV.

But they went cheap, and bought a fake leather sofa.
Yes, fake leather.
Fleather, I guess.

Now, the thing is, when they had me declawed, they only did the front claws, leaving me with my rear ones—for self defense, in case I ever need it. Like when they try to rub that stick thing over my teeth. The back claws really come in handy then. But when I jump, the force of my body weight bearing down before I spring up causes those back claws to come out a little bit. And if I jump off the sofa, or even onto it… Well, you can probably guess the result.

Fake leather does not hold up to kitty claws the way real leather does.
So there are teeny tiny holes in it.
And they've only had it for two weeks.

This is *so* not my fault. They should have a basic understand of feline physics, and should have thought the whole fleather thing all the way through.

Right?

The way I see it, by this time next year they're gonna be shopping for a new sofa, and maybe they'll get one that's a lot softer to sleep on. That fleather is cool, but dangit, a cat slides on it. And if a cat is sleeping on his back, with his head hanging over the edge, a cat winds up conking that head on the floor.

It's because they're cheap.
They are really, really, really cheap.

If they weren't, I'd have shrimp very night.
And kitty crack.
Shrimp and kitty crack.

November 29,2004

They brought a tree into the house again. I'm not going to get too excited about it, because I remember what happened last year when they brought a tree home—they got all pissy every time I tried to nibble on it, and then I did *something* (not sure what) and they took it away. And not in a nice way, either. The Man ripped it limb from limb and shoved the dead pieces into a box, right in front of me. It was horrifying to watch, and ever since then I've wondered what I did so wrong that made them take the tree away.

It doesn't taste as good as I always thought a tree would, but it's fun to hide behind and play with—lots of shiny, dangling things to bat at. Maybe if I'm really good this year, I'll get to keep it.

Or maybe they'll think this tree is prettier than the last one, and want to leave it right where it's at forever.

And perhaps monkeys will come flying out my ass, because we all know the odds of them doing something *I* want for any length of time.

If I had claws, I could make them leave it. Or leave a lot of their blood on the carpet as a reminder of the effort.

~ ~ ~

The People hate the vertical blinds that cover the glass patio door, but I think I really like them. If I run across the room and then dart behind them, it sounds like marbles going down wood stairs. Tons of marbles. This makes the people hate them even more, and that amuses me.

~ ~ ~

She bought a spray bottle.
A BIG spray bottle.
And when does she use this?
When I'm trying to sing her awake in the morning!

This morning I wandered back into the bedroom after the Man had fed me, and had barely opened my mouth, when she reached over for this blue bottle and aimed it right for me! Worse yet she pulled the freaking trigger and SQUIRTED ME!

I'm =this= close to never singing for her again.

~ ~ ~

In the old house, my bed was in the People's big bedroom, right next to the thing on the floor that blows warm air (and I miss that thing, let me tell you.) When we got here, it was put in the big bathroom—don't ask me why—and I never used it. Think about it—would you want to sleep near the place you poop?

Yesterday the Woman moved it from the bathroom to her office. It's not as nice as having it next to a steady stream of warm air, but at least this room doesn't smell like poop.

I hope she doesn't expect me to sleep in here at night. There's no way. I fully intend to spend every night draped across her legs, making them go numb.

Just because I can.

NOVEMBER 30, 2004

I did *not* have a bug up my ass, nor was I attacking everything in sight, no matter what the Woman claims. I was simply a little over excited; the Younger Human and his Much Better Smelling Friend came over tonight, and that got me going a little bit. Face it, they're young, they know how to play. My People...eh. Well.

Just when things were going really good—there was really good smelling stuff in the air, and yeah, I wanted some. So you know what the Man did? That bastard got out a thing of my treats and walked down the hall into the bedroom with it. He *knew* I would follow him. He gets me in there and gives me a scant few treats, and then he shut the freaking door! He locked me in the room! I could smell the real live fresh dead meat they were cooking, and I was pretty sure I could smell shrimp.

I swear, if there had been a phone in that room, I would have dialed 911. Or called the Cat Protection Society.

Later, like *forever* later, he let me out, and there was shrimp! A whole cut up piece of shrimp in a little bowl for me. I would have preferred two or three whole cut up pieces, but I think they ate the rest of them while I was locked up. Pretty freaking selfish, if you ask me. Some of it was in the *trash can*, for Pete's Sake. What sane person throws away perfectly good shrimp?

So after that, I *might* have gone a little berserk. And I *might* have jumped up and nipped at the Man once or twice or ten times, but it's not like I *bit* him. And I didn't draw blood or anything. I just ran around at top speed, jumping on things and people, and used my teeth a *tiny* bit. Just a tiny bit.

Hell, they thought it was funny.

Now that the Younger Human has left with his Friend, I've settled down and am going to go take a nap, so that I can sing joyously for the People at 3 a.m. in the bathroom, where my voice will echo for all to enjoy.

Because I'm just wonderful that way.

DECEMBER 1, 2004

The People had pork chops for dinner tonight, and the whole time they were in the oven (the pork chops, not the People) I could smell them and wanted one *so* much.

But I was good, I stayed out of the way, and only spoke up every 10 seconds or so.

Then, after dinner, the Woman was in the kitchen and she started cutting bite sized pieces off of a chop—and she gave it to me!

Pork!
Finally!
Real Pork!

And you know what?
It was awful.
I took one nibble and realized there's a reason pork is not put into cans of Stinky Goodness.

It. Just. Sucks.

The People have cleaned off the tops of the cupboards in the kitchen, and they weren't lying—I'm allowed to jump up there. It's a pretty cool view, but face it, it's not as much fun when they don't get ticked off.

They have a new china cabinet I'm not allowed to jump on…maybe I'll amuse myself by jumping up on top when the Woman can see me. She'll get all excited and her voice will get all high pitched, and she'll try to pull me down, but I know she's not tall enough. She'll grab a chair, but by the time she can get to me, I'll leap over her head, onto the counter, and up to the top of the cabinets.

Neener.
You can't catch me.

~ ~ ~

If we had a screen on the front door, the People could open it, and I could spend the evening watching bugs flock to the outside light. That's amusing in an odd sort of way; they fly up and bounce right off the light bulb, and about half of them wind up dead.

Don't they know that light bulbs get hot?
I know because I touched my nose to one once.
That'll never happen again…

DECEMBER 2, 2004

Ever since we moved (I still don't recommend it) the Man has been home every morning, and he gets up—without any prodding—and opens up a can of Stinky Goodness for me. Then he goes and reads the comics in the newspaper, and I wander to the bedroom, where the Woman is still asleep, and I sing to her.

She doesn't seem to appreciate this, but I still do it, because People need *some* culture, after all. Once I know she hears me (I know this because she either sighs really hard, or says, "Stop it, Max!") I go to the bathroom to use the litter box (no, I don't have to be delicate about it. A good meal precedes a good poop, and you know it) and then I go back and sing to her some more.

One of two things will happen. Either she'll threaten to throw something at me, or she'll get up. Well, actually if she threatens to throw something at me, she still gets up, but most mornings she doesn't threaten.

But…there's a giant Worry forming here.
The Man is home every morning.
This is not right.

Before we moved, most mornings he would get up very, very early (without feeding me) and leave. He'd come back later in the day, but just about every morning he went somewhere, and I *know* it has something to do with his ability to provide me with Stinky Goodness every day.

If he's here every morning, he's not doing whatever it is he does to get the Stinky Goodness.

Does this mean we're going to run out?
And what do I do if that happens?
I *cannot* exist on dry food alone!

The Woman has muttered something about "work" and "just a few more days," but I understand time—in a few more days I could starve to death. I don't understand *why* she's not making him get up and go out every day. Or for that matter, why *she* doesn't get up and go out every day.

I'll sing her awake every day, I really will.
Anything so I don't starve.

~ ~ ~

Hey.
Bacon is pork.
And bacon tastes good.
And when they have bacon, I get some.

So…this makes one wonder. If pork chops taste like ass, why does bacon taste so good? And if kitties probably shouldn't have pork, why do they give me nibbles of the bacon?

Most importantly, why do they have bacon so infrequently?
I mean, it doesn't cause flames to shoot out one's ass.
It's quite tasty.
It smells really good.

So why do they only have it a couple of times a year?
Why can't they just make it for me?

~ ~ ~

While the people were out, the doorbell rang. I was busy napping so it didn't bother me too much, but when they got back they said there was a tag on the door from the man in the brown truck.

That means *boxes*!

The only thing is, since they weren't home, he didn't leave it. So tomorrow they have to go someplace called "The Office" and get it.

I don't care what's in it—I just want the box!

~ ~ ~

Tonight there was another cat on the back patio; I stood by the door and tried to talk to him, but he just looked at me like I was speaking another language. He didn't move, didn't blink, just sat there like he was frozen in place, staring. Now I know I'm beautiful, but still... The polite thing to do is at least say Hello.

Maybe he was just shy. The Man heard me talking and came over to see what was up, and scared the other cat away, so if he had been about to say Hello he was scared out of it. You can't blame a cat for running when confronted with a giant human male of unknown origin. And temperament. If I didn't know the Man wouldn't chase me with a broom, I would have run, too. The worst the Man will do is pretend to hiss like a cat, but he doesn't know he sounds more pathetic than fierce when he does it.

After the other cat left, the People started talking. The Woman seems convinced that my trying to talk to the outside kitties means that I wouldn't mind having one inside. And that "come spring" they should think about getting a kitten.

EXCUSE ME?

I'm fairly sure the People talk to other people, but does that mean they should bring one of the Sticky Little Creatures home? *That* would fall into the category of When Hell Freezes Over...so why would I want a kitten? They're barely big enough to be more than snack sized, and I'm pretty sure they're not edible. Where would it sleep? Where would its box be? And most important, who would feed it?

Not me, that's for sure. I have a hard enough time getting these pathetic examples of human flesh to feed me, much less a baby kitty.

In fact, I'm not sure these People can be trusted with a baby *anything*. They already keep trying to sit on me—a baby kitty wouldn't be as fast or have as keen reflexes, and would probably become a kitty pancake within a week.

The People must be discouraged. "Come spring," whatever that is, they must be stopped. A baby kitty's life depends on it.

DECEMBER 3, 2004

Ok. It's two freaking twenty in the freaking morning, and the Woman is awake. She went to bed, turned out the lights, turned on her "special" music, and pulled the blankets up. But did she *stay* in bed? Hell no. Just as I got comfy on her office chair, the bedroom light flicked on, she shuffled down the hall to the kitchen for some of that really gross bubbly water she drinks way too much of, and then she came into the office.

And she picked me up and moved me from the chair—and then *thanked* me for warming it up for her.

People, look ... once you go to bed, *stay* there! Getting up disrupts your cat's routine, and makes them very, very irritable. And when cats are very, very irritable, something of yours is bound to meet a gruesome and toothy death. Or get slimed with a hairball. Or worse.

Don't say you haven't been warned.
And go to bed.
Your possessions depend on it.

DECEMBER 4, 2004

The Woman actually stayed in bed last night; I could have taken the opportunity to sleep in the office chair (it is pretty comfy, after all) but I decided to jump up on the bed with her to make sure she didn't get up. To add to that effort, I stretched out across her legs; this makes it difficult for her to move around, plus after a while her les get numb. If her legs get numb, she's not going anywhere.

I also didn't sing for her at 3 this morning, figuring she needed to make up some lost sleep. But did she appreciate that? Phfft. When I went in to wake her up this morning—a person shouldn't stay in be *too* late, after all—she *squirted* me! And worse yet, right about the time she aimed that squirt bottle at me, the Man came in to tell me to be quiet. Well, between the water and this giant mass of Human coming at me, I got a little bit startled and ran to the far side of the bed, where neither water nor human hand could get to me.

Those people just don't appreciate all I do for them.

I mean, if not for me, the Woman would be in bed all day. Or at least until 9 a.m., which might as well be all day. Lazy, lazy people…

DECEMBER 5, 2004

I got email today from some genius who felt some compelling need to complain about my "grammer." Yeah. That's how he spelled it. "Grammer."

Guess what, folks? I'm a cat. A self educated cat, I might add. I didn't get to go to kittygarden. I didn't have to suffer through preadolescent angst in middle school. I didn't have to pass academic competency tests to graduate high school.

Oh…and I'm only three freaking years old, too boot.

So I don't have the complete grasp of the rules of GRAMMAR, but at least I can spell better than can you.

Who sends email to a cat, anyway?

DECEMBER 6, 2004

The Man got up early this morning and left the house; I can only assume it means he finally went to pass gas so that he can buy more Stinky Goodness. At least I hope that's where he went. I looked under the sink this morning and we're almost out. There are only about 5 cans left, and I will not be happy if 6 days from now I have nothing to eat.

As soon as he left I went into the bedroom to let the Woman know, but she wasn't having any of it. She rolled over and put a pillow over her head, so I just jumped up on the bed and waited (sitting on her stomach, of course, so I'd know exactly when she was ready to be awake) – then the thing the People hold up to their ears and talk into started making noise, so she scrambled to get her glasses and pick it up before it stopped.

She didn't make it, though. She mumbled something about having to get it in case it was the Man needing help. I hate to point out the obvious, but the Man has been practicing and practicing, and he has passing gas down to a fine art. But while she was up, she opened a can of Stinky Goodness for me.

I greatly appreciated that, since it was technically a little early, so after I was done eating I went to find her and thank her, but she had gone back to bed. Well, I wasn't about to let that get in the way of good manners, so I thanked her loudly and profusely as I made my way to the litter box. I continued to thank her while I was in the bathroom, where my sweet voice echoes off the walls like fine, fine music.

She must have noticed my sterling behavior and manners, because she got up and made the bed. That was quite nice of her, since she knows that's my favorite napping place (and it's mine anyway, as evidenced by the giant fuzzy cat blanket that I allow the People to use at night.) She muttered things about going ahead and getting a start on the day ... I don't think she realizes, the day started off without her help and has been progressing just fine.

It's very quiet today, though, so I imagine I'll have to spend a good part of it talking to the Woman so she doesn't get lonely. I'd rather nap, but once in a while a cat has to do what a cat has to do.

Sheesh, the things we do for our People.
I bet she won't even appreciate it.

DECEMBER 7, 2004

Do the People think I'm stupid? Last night, after I'd plopped down on top of the Woman's legs for the twentieth or thirtieth time, she mumbled something about putting me outside.

Really now.
Sure she will.

And King Tut is going to spring to life and give us all a million bucks in pure gold.

This is the Woman who went tearing through the house, looking for me, on the off chance that I got outside because she caught a glimpse of a cat that sort of resembled me. Like she's really going to open the door and shove me outside. Where it's cold. And raining.

Not without my plastic tomb, she's not.
Or without a big fuzzy blanket, because I'm sure it's cold out there.

Oh, I got off the bed for a while, but not because I thought she would really do it.

I had to pee.

Really.

That was why.

~ ~ ~

If I'm asleep on the middle cushion of the sofa, and the Woman sits down (hard) on the end cushion, she can launch me off of it like a little kid flicks a booger off his finger.

I'm not sure I didn't like it…

DECEMBER 8, 2004

In the bathroom there's this little box that plugs into the wall; it's where the woman keeps some of her ~~drugs~~ medications. It looks a little like a tiny refrigerator, and keeps things cold like one, too.

Tonight I was up on the counter while she was ~~shooting up~~ injecting herself, and the door to it was open, and it looked like my head would fit right into it. And if my head looks like it's going to fit somewhere, I figure I'll see for myself.

I was right; my head fit perfectly and it is definitely very cold in that box. The Woman wasn't terribly amused, I don't think. She sighed and said that one of these days I'm either going to make her stick me with her needle by accident or I'm going to get my head stuck somewhere.

Yeah. I don't think it'll be an accident.

DECEMBER 9, 2004

The holidays are coming up.

Now, I don't know what that means, but the Woman said they are, and then said that I need to start thinking about what I want.

I want food on demand and an endless stream of kitty crack.

Haven't I established that like a million times already?

~ ~ ~

They changed my dry food again. The Woman says it wasn't on purpose, that the company that makes my dry food added hairball stuff to it.

What the hell. I don't need a hairball.

In any case, it's mostly tasty and I think I like it. It's not shrimp, but it'll do when Stinky Goodness isn't available.

But really…food with stuff for hairballs?
Has no one told people that cats can make those all by themselves?

If the Woman lets you into her closet, she can show you a really nice one I made for her just 3 or 4 nights ago that I don't think she's found yet…

DECEMBER 10, 2004

The Woman did not feel any pressing need to squirt me with that stupid water bottle this morning. Instead of standing by the door and singing to her, I jumped up on the bed and waited. I stood right next to her face, with my head hung low so that the first thing she would see when she opened her eyes was my beautiful face.

When she woke up, I learned that Jesus Christ is on a pogo stick, and she just lost 3 years off her life.

I'd like to see the guy on the pogo stick, personally.

DECEMBER 11, 2004

We have a really big bathroom, and I love to sing in there. My voice bounces off the walls, and I'm pretty sure the upstairs people can hear me. Since we can hear them pee, they have to be able to hear the melodious sounds of Max.

But my People just don't get it. I start singing, and the Woman comes back and asks me if I'm all right. And then she decides I must not like it being dark, so she flips the light on. Has no one explained to humans that cats can see in the dark? I don't need a night light in order to be able to find my litter box.

So she turns on the light…fine, I don't mind the light being on. Then I can see myself in the mirror—not that I sit there and stare, but it's nice to be able to see if I missed a spot while grooming. She leaves, I plop down and start singing again, and she comes back to double check. "Are you *sure* you're all right?"

Then she looks a me and decides I must not want to be alone, but "I'm sorry, I can't just sit in here with you."

Yeah, right. I've known the Woman to sit in the bathroom for a *very* long time. She could if she wanted, she just doesn't want to.

And I don't care.
I don't want her to.
I just want to sit in there and sing.

I may have to confine my singing to times when the People aren't home...they obviously have no appreciation for my talents, and no good ear for music.

Plus, I don't need them thinking they have to drop the pants and sit on the giant litter box just because I want to sing. That's just...wrong. Very, very wrong.

DECEMBER 12, 2004

It's really this simple:

If you don't want me to bite your head, quit washing your hair with stuff that smells like food.

~ ~ ~

Cookies straight out of the oven aren't as tasty as cookies that have sat there long enough to cool off. I think the People must already know this, because they didn't eat them right after taking them out of the oven, so there's no need for me to point it out. They'll eat them later, and by then not only will the cookies be cool, but any spit I left will have dried.

DECEMBER 13, 2004

Yes, that box of tissue *did* look a lot like a toy to me.
Problem with that?
If you go into the bathroom, we'll be having the same discussion about toilet paper.

December 15, 2004

I'm sitting on the special window seat, trying to peek through the slats of the window blind, when the Woman leans back and says, "Are you trying to look outside?"

Um, no, lady, I just like the dust on the freaking blinds.

"Do you want me to open them for you?"

Geez, don't take yourself away from your ~~literary masturbation~~ work to do me any favors, now.

And don't get your shorts in a wad when I walk away after you open them. The point is that they're open, not that I sit there and stare at the little rat-dog spend all day on a balcony in the next building. He won't jump anyway, and I have other things to do.

Like howl at the blinds to the patio, until you get up and open those, too.

16 December, 2004

I've decided that this is a kitty's bestest friend. The Woman brought it home a week ago, and ever since then it's been like having the special warm air blowing thingies we had in the floor of the place we used to live (here, they're up by the ceiling, where they do a cat no good.)

She put it in her office, probably thinking only of herself, but my bed is in there, too, and it's like a direct line from the warm thingy to my bed. I can curl up and be all toasty while I nap, and the Man is happy because it's cheaper than running the furnace.

I'd like to see that. I don't know what a furnace is, but if it's running to keep us warm, that's probably quite the spectacle. Maybe it has something to do with the people I keep hearing upstairs, even though I can't find any stairs to get up there and check them out.

Since Christmas is coming up (and now I know what it is, thank you for the emails, especially the ones that tried to make me feel stupid about it. Like a kitty is supposed to know about Christmas and Santa if no one tells him. But this year, I'm staying up all night and keeping an eye out for him, because I bet he has some primo kitty crack on him) I think all Cat Staffs should run out and buy these for the kitties.

We're worth it, you know.
We were once worshipped as gods.
Warm thingies should be our birthright.

December 18, 2004

Oh, man, you are so totally not going to believe it! One of the Sticky Little People was here! And it wasn't even one of these *wrong* medium sized foul mouthed Sticky Things that I see outside the window, it was one of the *right* Sticky Little People from the old place. I shit you not! I was minding my own business, and the People opened the front door, and there he was! Right in my own house!

Now, normally, a Sticky Person inside the house is a bad, bad thing. But I've been looking and looking for weeks, trying to figure out what happened to all the Sticky People I used to watch, and what do you know, the People brought one home for me. It was the little guy who lived right next door. He used to stand outside the screen door and play Peek-a-boo with me, and he learned to say my name before he learned to say a lot of other things.

He wasn't here for very long, though. And after I realized he wasn't in the house I went looking out the windows to see if he was playing outside, but I didn't see him. I'll keep looking, though. Maybe some of the other Sticky Little People will show up, too. I think I've missed them. They kept me entertained, especially when they'd throw a temper tantrum. There's nothing like a good Sticky Person temper tantrum.

It's dark out now so I'm pretty sure he won't be out there now, but I'll look again tomorrow.

December 19, 2004

I've been looking all day, and I can't find the Sticky Little Person.

If you see him, tell him to come back, because I want to watch him play outside my window.

Not that I miss him or anything…
It's the entertainment I miss.
Yep, that's it.
The entertainment.

December 20, 2004

You try to be nice, but what does that get you? A big lump of Grouchy Human with no appreciation for fine manners and delicate consideration.

I was *nice* to the Woman this morning. After letting her know the Man had left to go pass gas at 5:30 this morning, I settled down and waited for her to wake up. Well, when it was 10 minutes past breakfast time I was sure she must be starving so, I started singing to her. You know, nice, cheery holiday tunes that she could slowly wake to.

Did she appreciate this?

Phhft. She started off with "Be quiet, Max." And that was followed by "Enough, Max!"

Since she wasn't getting up, it obviously *wasn't* enough. So I continued with the private concert, singing at the top of my little lungs. Just when I thought she was going to get up—she sighed hard, like she does most mornings before crawling out of bed—she grunted, "Be quiet for five minutes, and I'll get up."

So I stopped singing. For five whole minutes. I know it was that long because I counted. One, two, three, four, five. She still didn't get up, so I started to sing again. Then she said, "Just TWO freaking minutes of quiet, okay?" So I counted to two before singing more.

I don't think the Woman can count very well.

Anyway, she finally got up, but instead of feeding me she puttered around, getting dressed, taking her drugs, scratching obscenely, and picking crap out from under her toenails.

I sang to her the entire time.
The Woman has no holiday cheer.
Grump, grump, grump.

One of these days I'm going to refuse to sing for her, and see how she likes *that*.

DECEMBER 21, 2004

The Woman bought a turkey! I saw it in the grocery bag; I even stuck my head in it and licked the wrapper. My tummy is all a-twitter (yes! I said it! A-TWIT-TER!) knowing that we're going to have real live dead turkey. I hope it's soon, because now that I know she bought one, I'm going to have dreams of eating turkey and other wonderful things.

I hope there will be shrimp, too.

Oohyeah. Shrimp and turkey.
Food of the gods.

DECEMBER 22, 2004

Why? Why does she do this?

The Woman went to bed early tonight; she watched TV for a little while and then turned out the light and turned on that music she listens to every night. Once I was satisfied she was done for the night, I wandered into the office to curl up on the chair, and sleep where there are no feet kicking at me "accidentally" as often happens when I sleep on the bed.

So 20 minutes later, here she comes, scooping me out of the chair to deposit me in my little bed. Now I like my little bed, but that's not where I was sleeping! I was sleeping in the *chair*. I had it first! And not only did she make me get out of the chair, after a few minutes she got up and left the room!

The nerve!

I'd go back to the bedroom and curl up there, but I know as soon as I do she'll decide she really is sleepy after all, and I'll wind up God knows where.

December 23, 2004

Well now, maybe the Woman will learn to not stay up so late at night. She was so sleepy today that she zonked out right after lunch, her head hanging off the edge of the bed. And her hair was just hanging down, waving in the air with each breath she took … so I decided it needed to be groomed. And as tired as she was, she wasn't going to groom herself. So I was nice and did it for her.

I don't think she fully appreciated my efforts, because when she got up and looked in the mirror, she started patting her head and muttering things like, "how did my hair get like this?" and "It wasn't wet when I laid down."

Well, no, but it got wet while you were snoozing.

I think she looks much better now. Like she stuck her finger in a light socket or something.

December 24, 2004

Our patio door is covered by these nifty plastic vertical blinds; the People hate them but I love them. So today while the Woman was talking into that thing she sometimes holds up to her ear, I got off her lap and sat on the end table, and started batting them around. She asked me to stop because she was on the phone with her mother, but I couldn't help myself. Those blinds are one of the most fun things ever. They almost make up for not having stairs to roll balls down anymore.

Later, I was running really fast through the living room, jumping over the counter to the kitchen, knocking things over. The People laughed but said I needed to clam down.

Calm down?
TOMORROW IS CHRISTMAS!!!

Ok, so maybe I didn't know what that was before, but after Googling and researching and reading Timothy's blog (timothydickens.blogspot.com) and what not, I get it. Tomorrow is presents for Max (I know because the Woman said I was getting a couple of presents) and boxes to play with, and TURKEY. Yes! The Woman is going to cook a real live dead turkey just for me! Well, I have to share it with the People, but mostly it's for me.

I'm not too sure about Santa...I mean, I don't like strange people coming into the house at all, but from what I understand, if I go to sleep early and stay in bed, he'll bring me something. So I'll go to sleep and take my chances. Though the Woman did say he only brings stuff to kitties that have been good.

I've been good.
Right?
So I get a present.
Right?
RIGHT?

I better go start singing to the People, just in case I need a little extra goodness on my side. We know how much they *love* it when I sing.

DECEMBER 25, 2004

I got presents! Santa brought me TWO things of crunchy treats. TWO of them! My favorite kinds! And the People gave me this ball that they can put crunchy treats in; if I roll it just right, the treats come out. It's kinda mean and kinda fun at the same time.

But I think best of all, there were boxes and paper and bags to play with.

They already got rid of the paper, but they left a lot of boxes for me to play with tonight. I think I'll do that after they go to bed.

And there was TURKEY! And SHRIMP!!! No kidding, I got my two favorite things to eat in the whole world today. The People taste tested it for me, to make sure it was good enough, so I waited very patiently on the kitchen floor, curled up on the little red rug in there. The Woman even said I was being very, very good. Which, if you think about it, was pretty spiffy of me, considering Santa had already come. I didn't get just a little taste, either. I got so much that I was really sleepy afterwards, and had to take a nap.

The Younger Human was here today, too. I think he took some of the turkey home with him, but the Woman said there was more and I would get some tomorrow.

Really, I'm still so full that I haven't even had my Stinky Goodness tonight, and I don't care.

This was just an awesome day!

DECEMBER 26, 2004

Ok. It was humiliating, but I had to do it. After all, the Woman gave me huge amounts of food yesterday, not to mention the presents, and the nice warm bed to nap in. The People deserve thanks of some sort, I guess, and the Woman in particular likes it when I do the cute thing, so I did.

I let her sleep this morning after the Man went to pass gas; I didn't announce that he'd left, and I didn't sing in the bathroom, even though I really wanted to. After all, I have a lot to sing about. But I let her sleep, and about half an hour before it was time for her to wake up to open a can of Stinky Goodness for me, I jumped up on the bed and curled up by her face, snuggling in tight. She calls it "spooning." I call it "feline humiliation," but she likes waking up to having me there snuggling with her.

She woke up quite happy and even fed me before she went to the giant litter box. And after, when she saw I was trying to bury myself in blankets on the bed, she turned the heat up for me, and told me to wait 5 minutes and the house would be warm. And it was!

Now, she better not expect me to do that every morning, but since I can't just go out and buy presents for people, that'll have to do.

Tomorrow we can go back to status quo; I will sing my little heart out at 3 a.m., and bounce up and down on the bed when I want her to get up to feed me.

I have a reputation to maintain, after all.
I wouldn't want people to think I was getting all cute and soft or anything.

DECEMBER 27, 2004

They left me alone *all day long*. It didn't just *seem* like it was all day—they left when the nice looking lady on TV was talking the news, and didn't come back until the old guy was talking the news. That's like a million hours, I think. If I hadn't needed to nap for most of it, I would have been mighty upset. And I would have been even more upset if they hadn't come home at dinner time long enough to feed me. Oh, they went back out, saying something about needing to go out and buy more cans of Stinky Goodness, but I was still alone. And it was getting dark. Okay, they did leave a couple of lights on, but still. They need to be home, where a kitty can find them, just in case he wants a lap, or a head skritch, or someone to sing to. Even if all he plans on doing is sleeping, because you never know when he might want one of those things.

DECEMBER 28, 2004

If a kitty is hungry an hour and a half early, and if that kitty has been good all night long, shouldn't that kitty be allowed to holler nonstop until SOME-ONE gets out of bed to open a can of Stinky Goodness?

I thought so.

It does no good to lie there stubbornly all that time and tell me to be quiet. I am going to win, no matter how long it takes.

DECEMBER 30, 2004

Um...if a person is in a bad mood, it is not a good time for a kitty to jump up on the table and scope out what their dinner is by sticking said kitty's face into the plate. A person in that bad a mood has NO sense of humor. AND they won't share.

DECEMBER 31, 2004

Happy Freaking New Year.

May the next bring lots of Stinky Goodness, shrimp, fresh live dead meat, kitty crack, and people who appreciate fine feline singing.

Yeah, I'm not holding my breath either.

The People

The Woman: K.A. Thompson. She's 43 years old, thinks she's a writer (but really, I think she spends most of her time playing online), and has written 3 novels. She is most appreciated for her opposable thumbs, because she is the one who mostly opens my cans of Stinky Goodness.

The Man: Mike Thompson. He's also 43 years old, recently retired from the United States Air Force, for whom he worked first as a registered nurse and then passed gas as a Nurse Anesthetist for a total of 20 years. He now works in Northern California, where he continues to pass gas, a job he very much enjoys.

The Younger Human: Curt Thompson, 21, college student. He's the one who brought me home. A friend of his had me first, but couldn't care for me, so when I was 4 months old he brought me to the People who would become my Staff. He's training to be an actor, and the People say he will be a very good one, and once he's rich and famous he can support them in the style to which they always hoped to become accustomed.

The Other People: the neighbors from Wright Patterson AFB in Ohio. They made my People happy while we lived there, and got them to consume massive quantities of Red Drinks.

The Sticky Little People: the offspring of the Other People. Jacob, Sammy, Patrick, Jonathan, Stephanie, Kimberly, Mercedes, Matthew, and Rhiannon. The view outside my window is just not the same without them there to amuse me.

And a special mention of my **Auntie Cookie**: Yes, Auntie Cookie, I have a potty mouth.

Visit my website at http://psychokitty.blogspot.com, and peek inside the Woman's head at http://kathompson.blogspot.com.

CPSIA information can be obtained at www.ICGtesting.com
Printed in the USA
BVOW081215211112

306137BV00003B/158/A